THE MIRROR

THOMAS KELLER

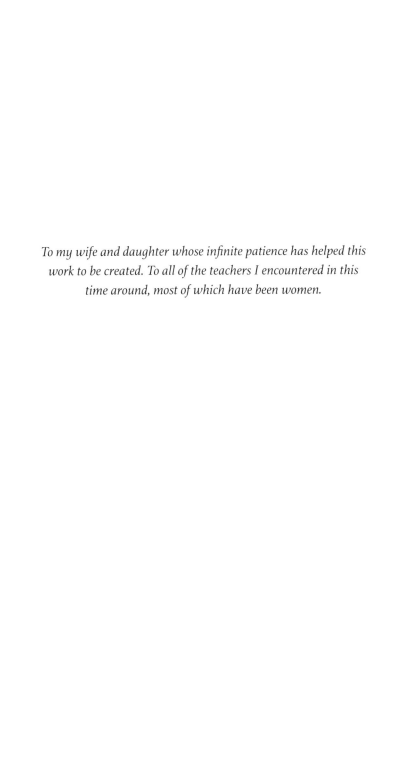

To my wife and daughter whose infinite patience has helped this work to be created. To all of the teachers I encountered in this time around, most of which have been women.

CONTENTS

THE BEGINNING

> If you want to make the world a better place
> Take a look at yourself, and then make a
>   change.
> —Michael Jackson lyrics from Man in the
>   Mirror

What you are about to learn took me forty-eight years to discover, even though this information has been available for hundreds of years. The concepts I'll explain appear prominently in Buddhism, Christianity, Hinduism, Judaism, Taoism, Zoroastrianism, along with the rest of the world's major religions, though it is most often cloaked in convoluted, elaborate language that makes it confusing at best and downright unrecognizable at worst. It incorporates a number of principles such as the Golden Rule (do unto others as you would have them do unto you) and the Law of Correspondence that states that our outer world is nothing more than a reflection of our inner world: as within, so without, as above, so below. It is grounded in the Law of Mentalism. It is also found within the phrase "birds of a feather flock together" when referring to groups of people and why they come together.

It is clearly saying that our current reality is a mirror of what is going on inside us. I have distilled the convoluted, confusing information into a simple three-step process called The Mirror.

This introduction is all fine and good but I'll go beyond this to explain how to use it to transform yourself into your finest being. The Mirror is not a religious practice and works regardless of your religious beliefs, or if you practice no religion at all. Using The Mirror will transform your blockages, your blind spots, releasing tremendous energy into your life and propelling you into your most fully realized self. I have simplified it to make it easily understandable and effective for you to use. I start very simply and throughout this book guide you through the process while giving you more and more advanced usage of The Mirror. What you will discover are the parts of you that have been holding back your love, peace, joy and success. And then you'll dissolve those parts completely, freeing up your energy and allowing you to move forward in your life effortlessly.

The Mirror is a simple yet profound process that can and will transform any disturbance, frustration, anger, or anxiety within you into peace and tranquility while freeing up your powerful life energy. Sometimes you'll be able to laugh at yourself and at other times it will hurt to see your hidden parts revealed. You'll probably even be shocked by what you discover within yourself. Ultimately those revelations and transformations will create the greatest growth for you. We will get through it together and transform all of it. Have courage. Be honest. And laugh whenever possible.

Laughing at ourselves makes this journey and work so much easier.

My Story

My mother used to say to me, "You came out of my womb looking for God." Of all the things to remember now some sixty-three years later! But looking back over my life, I believe she was right. The thing is, the God she was embracing at that time was one that sounded horrible. He was a "he," to begin with, and was very demanding and harsh. A God that said I was born a sinner and that's all there was to it, a God with lots of rules and thou-shalt-nots, a mean and cruel God whose only answer as to why some terrible things happen is that it is God's plan—so don't ask any questions. I can remember sitting in church at Sunday service when I was around five years old thinking to myself, "This is insane and what they are saying feels crazy." None of it made any sense to me or felt true in my heart, so I sat there until my mother said I no longer had to go. When she did I jumped out of that church, never looking back.

I do believe I came here looking for God. I attended every Easter service and tried numerous religions, always looking for something that felt right but finding nothing that did. I now call God Spirit because the term is inclusive of all religions and free-thinking people and doesn't carry so much baggage with it. The road I took to discover Spirit within myself was one of trying everything else until Spirit was all that was left. A process of elimination, if you will. But you don't need any religion or spiritual awareness for The Mirror to benefit you. That was just my journey of discovery. I encourage you not to take my word for this but to try it for yourself so you'll experience the benefits. Once you experience the benefits, you'll know exactly whether you like it or not.

I can still remember in my earliest days as a toddler, even up through six or seven years old, that I was aware of other beings around me who were not my parents or siblings but otherworldly beings. You can call them angels, guides, or etheric beings. I clearly remember having complete conversations with them. They were my friends; that's all I know. It was as if I had always known them. But I had parents and older brothers who found that ridiculous, and with a few smashes in the mouth and some ridicule I gave those conversations up completely. Around seven or eight years old I shut that down, deciding to no longer talk to or see my angelic friends, and faced the hard realities of the world I grew up in. I believe I went into survival mode. In complete frustration, I forgot any spirituality or shoved it so far back in my mind that it disappeared, or so I thought.

The more I looked around at and experienced life the more I became disappointed, frustrated, and scared. Scared? Yes, scared of a world that appeared to be chaotic, dangerous, and ruled by chance or random events. I saw a world that made no sense at all. Also, people were telling me what to do, when to do it, and what to believe, even when these things did not feel true in my heart. These people seemed so confident and assured me that their vision represented the way the world actually was and their way of doing things was what I needed to do to survive. People were lying, cheating, stealing, and worse—much worse. What the heck was I doing here! I don't belong here. Help!

As I grew into my teens and then twenties, I gave in to the ideas of conventional Western society: work hard, struggle, set goals, sacrifice to achieve, and buy, buy, buy. Shopping was always the answer. Anger was my go-to emotion. I didn't know why I was so angry. At the time I didn't even identify it as anger but I can see it so clearly now. I felt like I was on fire all the time.

Looking back now, I can see plenty to be angry about. I'd inherited a world of chaos where a person must grab everything they can. Chaos will instill tremendous fear, anger, and resentment. I was so angry that our way of living seemed to be all grabbing everything you can, taking it if you must, and holding on to it for dear life. Much of my anger has been resolved over the years using The Mirror, but some still remains. It's as if anger is such an ingrained habit that I jump to it when frustrated—with traffic, for example. I'll continue with this issue throughout this book, but first let me give you a fuller picture of my life growing up.

I grew up in middle-class, Midwestern America. My parents were very loving and angry people. Yes, it is possible to be both at the same time. They certainly did everything in their power to provide my siblings and me with a good upbringing. They provided plenty of opportunities and a good education. Their way of discipline involved not "sparing the rod so as not to spoil the child." Corporal punishment episodes occurred regularly. I wasn't singled out: the discipline was distributed evenly among us siblings. My dad owned his own business and participated in our lives, coaching Little League and swim team. Mom was loving, supportive, and a mess of worry. I have two older brothers with whom I fought constantly.

Yet there were lovely parts: I grew up in a charming Southern town in the countryside, which created a beautiful and lasting bond with nature that it is still in me. We lived just a short drive from the stunning Kentucky Lake and the Land Between the Lakes National Recreation Area. I cherished the beauty and peace I felt there. This area has thousands of trees blanketing rolling hills that extend right down to the edges of numerous lakes. Nature is what I return to frequently when I need help or I'm feeling stressed out. I can take a walk in nature and whatever had seemed so stressful before diminishes in my mind. In a natural environment I don't have to meditate, chant, or hike to feel better. It's as if nature is working on me just because I'm there. Nature is my church, you could say.

WHAT IS LIFE REALLY ABOUT?

> Each person you meet is an aspect of
>   yourself, clamoring for love.
> —Eric Micha'el Leventhal

My family could be called a typical American family. As I grew into my teens, I realized that the underlying message being taught to me was always about getting *safety*: be safe, stay safe, protect yourself, be afraid of strangers, watch your back, life is dangerous. Safety is the Holy Grail in Western society.

The implications are wide: safety means having lots of money, which means a career that makes a lot of money. So that dependable career where you can earn a steady paycheck every two weeks ensures your safety, and never mind about working at something that sparks your imagination or something you find inspiring.

The second big area where safety is needed was in a romantic relationship. No one meant just any relationship; safety extended to one that lasts until death do us part so that I never have to look for a spouse again. That marriage would make me safe because I would be taken care of for the rest of my life, but safety also required getting health insurance to pay for my ill health as I age. Safety, safety, safety. Safety was always about money and money was always about safety.

Millions of Americans believe money equals safety and that is their earthly purpose. Oh, they may say God is first, or their particular religion is first. But their actions say money is first and then comes everything else. That recipe for fulfillment has been proven empty time and again. I know from first-hand experience: I had a lot of stuff and very little fulfillment. I was filled with fear regardless of the amount of money I had. I would celebrate when a big bonus arrived or I sold a property, only to count down in fear as the dollars got spent and the bank balance of safety went down, down, down.

I wasn't alone in this way of thinking. So many people achieve wealth and believe this will make them feel secure only to be left feeling empty. A sense of fulfillment grounded in material things is fleeting. There are many stories about people who have achieved wealth, fame, and high honors only to feel that something is still missing. How many millionaires live in fear they'll lose it or people will try to take it away from them? How lonely it is to always be suspicious of other people's motivations. How insecure it is to be always counting the dollars afraid of not having enough money to live out a life being well cared for.

Now, I am a big fan of money and having plenty of money is a lot more fun than not. But my story is about moving beyond the number of dollars one has and mastering what creates those dollars in the first place. So if safety alone is enough for you, then this book is not for you.

It is predicted that in 2019 approximately 50% of all

marriages will end in divorce. No safety there. And 66% of all businesses fail within the first ten years. No safety there. And how many stories of fraud have you heard about in retirement funds, 401Ks, and other financial investments? Little safety there.

The problem with safety as we advance in the game of life, advance in consciousness, is that safety becomes a trap. It's a box that gets smaller and smaller each time we try to be "safe." Safety becomes imprisonment and stops us from ascending in consciousness because there's a great tendency to believe safety is the end of the game. There's a tendency to stop being creative, thinking out of the box, allowing inspiration to come through and being willing to follow that guidance.

So don't allow yourself to be trapped in safety. I am talking about living a life where one is free to have everything and do anything. A life where one can live anywhere, work anywhere or not at all. A life of freedom. Safety comes within that, but it's a different kind of safety than what we're typically taught about in America. There is a place beyond safety concerns where freedom can be found. This is freedom from counting your dollars, freedom from budgeting your dollars, freedom from buying a lesser item than what you really wanted because you thought you couldn't afford it. Freedom to do what you want, travel where you want, move through your life fulfilled and free in your heart. Freedom to be guided into relationships and know that the person in front of you is the right person for you now. And most of all, freedom where there is no fear.

What I am sharing in this book is my real-life journey and the realizations that have moved me from safety to freedom. Freedom is the true Holy Grail.

This story traces the continuing evolution of my life. In

my twenties and thirties, I lived in Los Angeles and was a general contractor making great money. Yet I had no relationship, little inspiration, and was continuing my search for real meaning in my life. I was pursuing the "American Dream" and could already sense it would be a hollow victory. The more money I made, the more empty I felt. I could sense money was not going to bring happiness but the idea was so ingrained in me that I couldn't get out of the money = success mindset. But once I'd achieved what I thought was financial success, the hollowness of the triumph quickly became obvious.

I then began to reassess my life. I seemed to be quite talented. It appeared that I had a good brain and excellent physical skills. So why was I feeling so empty and off? I was achieving and being successful in business.

As I look back over my life I can now see that I would begin one thing after another, becoming quite good at each skill and achieving a lot of success only to be left feeling empty. In my early twenties I was a professional board sailor, traveling to competitions from Hawaii to the mainland. After that I turned to construction contracting. This pattern occurred over and over until I was able to see that no matter what I was pursuing, it just wouldn't work because there was a link missing within myself. Thank goodness that in one of the darkest times in my life I clearly heard a voice within myself telling me that I was good and that I should keep searching for truth because I would find it. I have never forgotten that voice and I trust in it all the time.

After repeating the pattern of mastery and disappointment, I came to the realization that the missing link wasn't in my physical abilities or intelligence. So I began to look inward. I read self-help books such as "The Road Less Traveled" and writings by Joseph Campbell and Carlos Castaneda. I went to a psychologist, and after a couple of sessions she said that I understood everything she was talking about and that there was no need to continue paying her for visits. She suggested that I attend a metaphysical church named Agape, a transdenominational church in Los Angeles teaching new thought, ancient wisdom. I did this for many years and continued to grow. I also attended many workshops by personal growth experts and even walked on fire in a week-long event in Hawaii. All seemed helpful but that help only lasted a short time because goal-setting and marching ahead wasn't what was missing for me.

I've always been a truth-seeker. I did feel I had glimpses of what I was searching for; the Agape Church and teachings of Universal Law gave me my first clues. Then a guest speaker at the church named Teri MacBride lit a fire under me with his loud, bold, and direct talk of his illness, recovery, and spiritual experiences: that was the second clue. I traveled to learn about the ancient cultures of Peru, Mexico, Belize, and Guatemala; I visited the Serengeti Plains by way of Kenya; and took seven trips to Egypt studying the ancient temples. That busted the doors wide open.

I'd come to the realization that what was missing for me was my spiritual connection. By pursuing this realization I discovered aspects of the Law of Mentalism and the Law of Correspondence. (Let me just repeat that The Mirror works for everyone, regardless of any religious or spiritual beliefs.) When I began studying with Dr. Carolyne "Isis" Fuqua, a teacher of Egyptian mysticism, A Course of Miracles and the founder of Circles of Light Ministries, I discovered more power to transform my life. Dr. Carolyne leads groups of people all over the world through life-transforming evenings, retreats, and purposeful journeys to sacred places as part of her traveling ministry. A master teacher of Egyptian mysticism, Dr. Carolyne grounds her teaching in Universal Law and metaphor, which are the keys to unlocking the memory of our true purpose. I have placed a link in the back of this book for you to discover more information about her.

In the early 2000's I discovered the Universal Laws of Mentalism and Correspondence and that led to Mirroring. As stated earlier I have simplified the process down to three steps making it easy to use and comprehend. Until the age of forty-seven, I'd had few relationships and no long-term ones. I was a real loner and didn't think I would find my soul mate—or any mate. I had been using The Mirror for about a year when I met my wife-to-be. We are a mixed-race couple and I thought I was clean of any racism. But when I got into a deeper relationship with her I saw ugly racism was still within me. What I saw within myself were harsh judgments against white males such as myself. I judged them as greedy, undermining, and willing to sacrifice everything to get money. I worked with The Mirror to dissolve these judgments and I will talk about these judgments later because they created a life threatening illness in my body.

I used The Mirror actively and with intensity because I loved this woman and I knew I did not want to be a racist person. I was shocked to discover the prejudice within me, but I stuck with The Mirror and transformed it. My wife and I have been together fifteen years. The first few were very tough on us: we had a lot of work to do to discover and heal our fears and judgments. We persisted by using The Mirror and worked it out. We now have an amazing thirteen-year-old daughter and a relationship that continually becomes deeper and richer.

I went from being a loner, only taking care of myself, to

providing for a family. And just as important is the type of person I've become in that process of creating a deep intimate relationship with my wife. I'm now a person who cares for others, not just myself, and I'm willing to grow, to expand, to stretch myself because of the use of The Mirror. My wife and I both use The Mirror as our primary parenting and relationship tool. There are stories of parenting to follow in this book.

As I remember the twisting path I took to become my best self, I recall spiritual and religious teachings that contained this information. But it was always cloaked in lofty, convoluted language creating confusion for the student. The Mirror works for anyone, anywhere, anytime. Again don't take my word for it. Try it and see for yourself.

MEET THE MIRROR

> Our language is the reflection of ourselves.
> —Cesar Chavez

What I'll be sharing with you is a simple, profound, and sometimes deeply disturbing tool that is grounded in Universal Law. It's simple in that there are only three steps. It's profound in that it will instantly change your life and always for the better; it will always work. It can be deeply disturbing in that sometimes you won't believe what you will see about yourself. Your conscious mind won't show you the hidden blind spots that are holding you back, but by using The Mirror, your subconscious mind will. You may try to deny The Mirror, distance yourself from it, be appalled by it, but the truth is it will always be you and will always be there for your benefit, should you choose to use it. The beauty is that the third step of The Mirror process will dissolve any frustration and disturbance and send you into freedom and joy, releasing vibrant energy into your life. Specifically, you'll have access to more life energy, that is yours to use. A key point to remember is that "forgiveness" is not what you were taught it is, and certainly not what 99.9% of the world thinks it is.

It is within our relationships that the greatest gifts of transformation reside. It is only through our interactions that we can truly know ourselves. I know that I personally ran from relationships until I turned about forty-five years old. I claimed that I was a loner, a free bird. Oh, I had romantic relationships for a short time and then they would fall apart. I had a couple of close friends who fell away as I moved time and time again. Being a lone wolf didn't hurt me as long as I didn't desire more for my life. But once I did desire more, that desire propelled me to search, learn, and discover more. I realized that if I was meant to be an enlightened one meditating in a cave or on a mountaintop for years, I would not have been born in the United States. Meditation is great, powerful, and very helpful, but I was born not to hide away and meditate.

I was born to go forward though my issues, not to avoid them. If you're alone, there is no one to show you your blind spots. You know: the areas where we tell ourselves we're fine, but our results speak otherwise. Or we keep hitting the same wall ad infinitum only to repeat the error yet again. The good news is we don't have to repeat these blind spots any longer. But we do need relationships to work with The Mirror. They can be casual or serious, friendly or confrontational, but we must have relationships. Adios to the lone wolf.

It is in your relationships that all you blind spots reside and if one spends most of their time alone there's no one to show your blind spots. My wife often talks about how her life was so peaceful before she met me. To her credit, she did have a previous marriage and most likely relished the time alone after the turmoil of ending a marriage, regardless of the circumstances. She and her dog lived in a condo and she loved her time alone. It might have been a time of incubation and maybe that's exactly what's needed for a while. After we met, her life was in transformation as we reflected to each other the blind spots that needed to be transformed so we could really live a peaceful, passionate, and free life. Spouses, children, friends, co-workers, and bosses are all there for our benefit if we choose to use those interactions for our growth and freedom.

So what else besides relationships is needed to succeed at this adventure called life? Faith? No. I'm not talking about having faith in something you can't see, hear, feel, taste, or touch. You don't have to trust this process. You just have to do it and see your own results. Gather your own evidence. As you begin applying The Mirror you will see evidence that clearly demonstrates your movement in the direction of more and more freedom. Faith and trust are unnecessary. The willingness to use The Mirror is all that is needed to enjoy the results. You'll witness what works and collect the evidence for yourself. You're in charge. Courage is a big help, so be strong and honest with yourself and be willing to dig a little deeper into your thoughts. This is for people who are willing to go deep and that have a desire to uncover the truth of their life.

You'll become the Sherlock Holmes of your own life because the evidence of success is very real. Holmes methodically studied the details, paying attention to everything. That's what you must do: look at your life scientifically. Don't deny the evidence around you. If you see an aspect of being in another person, know that it is in you. Deduction is your greatest tool here. Look honestly at the people around you: are they honest or liars, generous or thieves, givers or takers, well or sick, happy or depressed?

Are they sick or alive? Don't always listen to what they say they are, but look at their behaviors, which will tell you everything you need to know. Actions truly do speak louder than words, and you need to be scientific to uncover the truth.

Holmes was the first detective to use the scientific method to solve crimes intelligently; before Holmes, the police rounded up the usual suspects and roughed them up looking for a confession. Police work had been crude and unscientific. Sir Arthur Conan Doyle kept up to date with current medical and scientific advancements. As a result, his fictional character Sherlock Holmes was at the forefront of the early CSI movement.

Holmes began at a crime scene by examining the evidence in detail. With each piece of evidence he examined, he came closer to the truth. His critical analysis of the evidence was cumulative: each fact would pile on top of the last, building to the truth. Holmes said when everything else is eliminated, what's left must be the truth, no matter how unbelievable. We must take this position with ourselves when using The Mirror. You will get great results and the results will compel you forward because you see and feel the energy being freed up as you transform your own consciousness.

This universe has a set of laws that, when worked by you, will work for you consistently. It's always about your consciousness. As you begin to apply this information you will gather evidence and as the evidence piles up, your journey will accelerate like a snowball growing larger and rolling faster down a hill. Interrogate yourself and witness that when you did a certain thing, a certain result happened. You'll become a witness to your own growing freedom.

THE THREE STEPS OF THE MIRROR

> Everyone and everything that shows up in
>   our life is a reflection of something that is
>   happening inside of us.
> —Alan Cohen

Step 1: Perception/Projection

Perception/Projection, the first step to freedom, is your mind creating or projecting like a film projector. It is constantly and always projecting the film of your current consciousness. The physical world is the screen your consciousness is projecting onto. Projection is what you see and participate in, minute by minute, every day of your life. Projection is the people in front of you such as your spouse, children, friends, co-workers and bosses. So if you really want to move from safety to freedom you must pay attention to what you are projecting onto your life's film screen, the world in front of you. I bind perception and projection together because in this work they are the same, so I'll be using the word *projection* to mean perception from now on because it drives home the point more directly.

Whatever I am projecting from my consciousness—both consciously and subconsciously—shows up as the people, attitudes, and qualities of people in my physical world. Okay, take a breath. I'll walk you through this step by step scientifically, so you won't have to guess. This is a very practical book with tools you can use immediately to improve your life. I don't want you to take my word for anything in this book. Try it and see for yourself. Experiment with this so you can see that you are creating your life and creating the way people respond to you.

Your consciousness is being projected out, as the film you see, the world you experience. Take a minute and think about the people most prevalent in your life now. Think about what their qualities are, their characteristics. Now pick one person that you admire, who's close to you but not your spouse. (We don't start with our spouse because typically there are too many emotions involved for us to be able to see clearly.) Pick someone close to you, and look at that person now. Be brave. What do you admire most about this person? Is this person honest, generous, faithful, supportive, strong, clear, compassionate, helpful, creative, intelligent? Pick just one quality and write it down in the space below with the person's name. I'll do one first as an example:

Projection

Question: What is S.J.K. saying or doing that I most admire?

Answer: S.J.K. just blows me away with her generosity.

Now it is your turn to select someone you know well and respect.

Projection

Question: What was this person saying or doing that I most admire?

Answer: _Talking chances_

This person is a clear film that you're projecting your consciousness onto, projecting from your consciousness into the world. Now look inward, toward yourself, and ask yourself this question: Where do you exhibit the same quality you wrote down about the person that you admire? My example looks like this:

Reflection

Question: Where do I say or do the same thing I admire about S. J. K.?

Answer: Even though I can put on a tough exterior face, the truth is that I will and do help anybody, at any time, without a second thought. S.J.K. is showing me the generosity that's within me. I see for myself how generous I am at work by doing much more than is being asked or required.

Now it's your turn to take a look at that person you know and reflect upon yourself to answer this question.

Reflection

Question: Where do I say or do the same thing as this person I admire?

Answer: _Toustmastens_

Don't rush this. Take all the time you need. This is the beginning step, so be thorough with this. One thing to consider here is that acting and thinking are equivalent in this process. I'll talk more about this later. For now, do the same process for two more of your closest friends. Write down your answers.

Projection

Question: What is this person saying or doing that I admire?

Answer: *Being Kind*

Reflection

Question: Where do I say or do the same thing as this person?

Answer: *Whenever I meet someone new*

Projection

Question: What is this person saying or doing that I admire?

Answer: *Being a good listener*

Reflection

Question: Where do I say or do the same thing?

Answer: *At 7 PM, or when someone is speaking.*

Take a moment to really appreciate what your friends are showing you about yourself. Then deeply appreciate these qualities within yourself. Appreciation (a form of gratitude) is such a powerful, life-transforming quality. Appreciation alone will increase the quality of your life tremendously, so take the time to appreciate the positive qualities you have discovered and own them for yourself. Gratitude is one of the most powerful energies in the universe. Being in a state of gratitude will, by itself, transform your life. Bask in your gratitude and remind yourself often that you are the positive qualities that you see in others because you are the projector. Gratitude alone is very transformative and now scientific research confirms this.

Published research summarized in a white paper prepared for the John Templeton Foundation by the Greater Good Science Center at UC Berkeley in May 2018 states:

Individual Benefits of Gratitude Research suggests that gratitude may be associated with many benefits for individuals, including better physical and psychological health, increased happiness and life satisfaction, decreased materialism, and more. A handful of studies suggest that more grateful people may be healthier, and others suggest that scientifically designed practices to increase gratitude can also improve people's health and encourage them to adopt healthier habits. In general, more grateful people are happier, more satisfied with their lives, less materialistic, and less likely to suffer from burnout.

Gratitude may also benefit people with various medical and psychological challenges. For example, one study found that more grateful cardiac patients reported better sleep, less fatigue, and lower levels of cellular inflammation, and another found that heart failure patients who kept a gratitude journal for eight weeks were more grateful and had reduced signs of inflammation afterwards. Several studies have found that more grateful people experience less depression and are more resilient following traumatic events. Research suggests that gratitude inspires people to be more generous, kind, and helpful (or "prosocial"); strengthens relationships, including romantic relationships; and may improve the climate in workplaces. Gratitude is also important to forming and maintaining social relationships. For example, one study found that participants who were thanked for helping a student on an assignment were more interested in affiliating with that student in the future; another study found that partners who had a series of conversations expressing gratitude to their partner reported more improvements in their personal well-being and in the well-being of their relationship than did partners who had conversations disclosing something personal about themselves. Though there has not been a great deal of research explicitly focused on gratitude in the workplace, a handful of studies suggest that gratitude may help employees perform their jobs more effectively, feel more satisfied at work, and act more helpfully and respectfully toward their co-workers.

I can not overstate how, by just focusing on gratitude, your life will become sweeter and sweeter. The positive qualities you see in your friends and family are great because they are you. Yet the greatest transformation in your life will come when you turn The Mirror on the things that disturb you the most about the people around you.

What I want to deliver to you is a method for recovering the energy back into your life from the "blind spots:" unconscious thoughts that are dragging you down. This is what's causing you to create the same relationship no matter how many partners you try. Those blind spots cause you to create the same problems with your boss or fellow workers, regardless of how many companies you move through. The things that disturb the most about your friends, spouse, parents, siblings, and children are within your consciousness. These things are holding you down and stifling your energy to create the life you desire because you are not consciously aware of them yet. If you were aware of them, you would have already done something about them! So dig deeper and become scientific about the information you gather.

A story from my life will give an example.This is critically important because as you recognize yourself in the people around you and do The Mirror work, you will gain the evidence that this is working and releasing pent up energy into your life. That will give you the confidence to continue forward bravely into your bold new world of freedom.

"The Mirror in the Parking Lot"

I live in Southwest Florida, and the difference in traffic between seasonal traffic and off-season is dramatic. Traffic triples from December to May and the driving style runs the gamut: New York City drivers, drivers from the countryside of the Midwest, Canadian drivers, and drivers from all points in between.

When I first moved to S.W. Florida, I was parking at Whole Foods during the beginning of the busy season. Traffic had been swamped all day and I had been driving a lot, but I believed I was peaceful and thought I was going with the flow. As I pulled into the Whole Foods parking lot, I said to myself, "What a relief to park after such a day of driving." I was then adjusting my parking spot by moving in reverse and then pulling forward. What I didn't see was a young man walking behind me. He yelled obscenities at me, catching my attention.

This was the first time experiencing the crush of driving during busy season. I immediately yelled back and became enraged. He responded aggressively and we went back and forth a couple of times finally agreeing to go our separate ways while grumbling. At least I was grumbling.

After a couple of minutes, I calmed myself down, took a few deep breaths and started using The Mirror—step one was remembering that I am the projector and doing my work of seeing how he was a reflection of me since I am the projector. I recognized he was showing me how truly stressed I was trying to adjust to all the newfound traffic. I had been telling myself I was fine and going with the flow, but The Mirror was showing me that I was stressed and angry. I took a deep breath and embraced this truth. I took a couple more deep breaths and admitted to myself that I had been very frustrated with the traffic.

I was then able to relax and laugh a little at myself. I was so disturbed at this young man cursing at me that I forgot he was showing me my real state.

I now know that the traffic will change greatly in the winter here and I'm no longer surprised by that. Since that one incident, I haven't had any problems driving during the busy season or the off-season. Sometimes just knowing something—just becoming aware of it—is enough to change it.

This is a simple story of Perception/Projection that demonstrates the first step of The Mirror. It is a clear example of what a blind spot looks like and how The Mirror works. What I had been telling myself as I was driving around in heavy traffic was that I was calm and cool. But what my Projection, the young man in the parking lot, swearing at me, was showing me was I was tense, frustrated and stressed out. The internal voice will sometimes tell us one thing but The Mirror will always show us the truth. The two can be quite different at times, but The Mirror always tells the truth.

THE MIRROR REFLECTS:
STEP TWO

> The secret is in discovering what you were
>   not conscious of before. If you had been
>   aware of it before, you would have already
>   done something about it. One must desire
>   the deeper truth.

Step Two: Reflection

Your consciousness is projected out and then reflected back to you by the people in your life. You can often only see your conscious and subconscious thoughts/beliefs out pictured by observing these people. Reflection is whatever is being said to you and done to you by the people closest to you. Think of them as being on a movie screen and you, the projector/consciousness is writing their script moment by moment. Reflection is what your spouse, mom, dad, siblings, friends, and close relationships are showing and saying to you while in front of you.

While in front of you is critical because a person can be different in front of different people, depending on the observer's consciousness. Have you ever noticed that you and another person can hold completely different opinions of the same person? That's because that person you share in common is reflecting different things according to each observer's consciousness.

I have a very good friend who, for the longest time, my wife has found annoying; she said he was an agitator. She didn't want to be around him because of this. I have never had that experience of him, but he did tell me stories about doing things that would catch people off-guard. I thought it was part of his sense of humor. He told me he thought he was being funny. I didn't and still don't see him as an agitator. He was clearly being different when with my wife and me, and reflecting our own unique consciousness.

It is in our relationships/reflections that we discover our blind spots and therefore find out what to work on in ourselves. Step one is Projection. Step two is Reflection. Projection is your consciousness (including your subconscious mind) projecting out; that's Step One. Reflection is that projection being shown to you in your relationships, and that's Step Two. Relationships are so valuable for many reasons and specifically here because they show us what we need to transform. I will repeat myself a few times to allow that to sink in so please don't be offended.

Who do you talk to regularly? Who's closest to you? It's your spouse, family, friends, co-workers, employees, bosses, and people you know or with whom you come into contact. Your mind projects your consciousness outward and then these people are the screens in physical form, reflecting what you think and believe both consciously and subconsciously.

How does your mom or dad or spouse treat you? Are they bossy, telling you what to do and how you should live?

That's a direct reflection of your own bossiness. That's your consciousness coming out of their mouths. If it's something you don't like hearing, it is most likely your own subconscious beliefs. How does your husband or wife or best friend interact with you? Are they loving or demeaning, supportive or undermining, secretive or open? Your consciousness is being reflected back to you all the time.

How about the friends closest to you? Are they generous or cheap? Are they inclusive or exclusive? Are they respectful or do they gossip about others? They are showing you your own consciousness. Do you have friends who are thieves, liars, or worse? If you have a friend who steals, take a look at where you steal or you are a "taker"—because thinking about doing something and actually doing that thing are the same in our consciousness.

Birds of a feather really do flock together. Does someone in your life complain a lot? That means you are a complainer. But perhaps you tell yourself you are not. And maybe you don't complain out loud—but how about in your head? Each person in your life is going to show you information about your real beliefs, both conscious and unconscious. Be brave when looking, because it is the things you don't like, the things that disturb you the most, that will provide the greatest rewards to you when you complete The Mirror process. These things, when forgiven in Step Three, will give you the greatest freedom and growth.

It can be hard to see your role in some of these reflections. Your ego will rant and rave, declaring that this could not possible be you, but, if you dig a little deeper in your thoughts, you will find it and you can use that to free yourself releasing tremendous energy into your life. When you see a reflection in another you may say to yourself, "That's crazy. That's not me." Well, good. Because that reaction shows that you have a lot of disturbance on the issue and the amount of disturbance is equal to the amount of freedom you'll gain when you complete The Mirror process. The bad news is that as long as you complain about it you're not done with it. Identifying the issue is half the battle. The good news is that you could be free of it very soon.

Everything the people around you show you, good and/or bad is a reflection of your consciousness. I can't say that too many times because it really needs to sink in and again don't be offended by my repetition of these ideas. There can be a lot of resistance to this idea but if you look objectively, like Sherlock Holmes would, you will begin to see it. In the next exercise we'll begin to see ourselves more deeply and clearly. Do this exercise by answering the questions as honestly as possible. I'll do one as an example first.

Projection

Question: What was this person saying or doing that disturbs me?

Answer: S.J.K. is so stubborn and never listens to my suggestions.

Reflection

Question: Where do I think or act like that, completely disregarding other people's suggestions?

Answer: Oh, my. I didn't have to look far in my mind. I must admit I often believe my way is the best way and things have to happen my way even when other suggestions are good.

Now it's your turn to answer the questions. Think of someone close to you but not your spouse (you'll save your spouse for later, since we generally have too many emotions and attachments to be able to work with a clear mind when it comes to our spouse). So maybe pick a regular friend or a co-worker. You already know the person I'm talking about, so use that one. I know there are a lot of things you already like about this person; and you can appreciate those aspects in yourself. But the big growth for you will come from what disturbs you about him/her. Now think of the one thing that most disturbs you about this person. Does this person lie, gossip, talk negatively, steal, judge people? Being as honest with yourself as possible, what is the one thing she/he does or says that disturbs you most?

Projection
Question: What is this person saying or doing that disturbs me?
Answer:_____

_____

Reflection
Question: Where do I say or do the same thing, or think about saying or doing it?
Answer:_____

_____

What did you come up with? Can you see where you're doing it? Remember that in this exercise, just wanting to do that negative act counts as much as actually doing it. Our thoughts are creative and they create our conditions and experiences. We want to write these things down to clearly identify and ground ourselves into the moment and the work we're doing. But you don't have to write down the name of the person that reflected the information to you, if you don't want to; just the quality or behavior.

That may have been a lot to take in. So stop, take a couple of deep breaths, and keep an open mind. Great work. We work with the things that disturb us because that's where our blind spots are. Also that happens to be where all the growth and freedom will be released in your life once you complete using The Mirror.

It's like having a pain in your back that persists for so long that you become used to living with it and think that's just the way life is for you. Now let's say one day something happens to you and the pain is removed from your body. You instantly feel so much better, so much lighter and more free. You can't believe you lived with the pain for so long. You had forgotten how good it is to feel good. You have more energy and therefore more fun. Your whole attitude is lifted: life looks better. The quality of your life increases across the board.

Here is one of my favorite true-life stories demonstrating how projection and reflection can work over three generations.

"The Three Mirrors"

For all of our fourteen-year relationship, my wife would get greatly offended by a particular tone of my voice that I would use toward her in very specific moments. In her words, she felt that I was condescending with a touch of dismissiveness, implying that she was an idiot. I could literally say two words to her in a particular tone of voice and she would get so upset. For example, we were checking out of a hotel in Orlando, Florida, and she wanted to drop the keys at the office. I said something like, "Why don't you leave them in the room?" What she heard was, "You are so stupid. Just leave them in the room." She was incensed with my response. I literally couldn't see how I was being so offensive and would tell her that insulting her was not my intention at all. I honestly was blind to it.

And for all of our fourteen-year relationship, I, in turn would be greatly offended when my wife made a very particular response to something I would say. I saw her as being condescending with a touch of dismissiveness, implying that I was an idiot in her response to me. Her response might be one or two words or even just a particular look, and I would recoil. She didn't understand why I was so offended and assured me that was not what she meant. I'm positive it was never her intention to come across this way.

This went on from time to time for thirteen of our fourteen years together. This past year we were visiting her mother across the country in California. The three of us were having a casual conversation in the kitchen one evening when my wife asked her mother a simple question. Her mother turned from the stove to face my wife and gave her "the look". Her mother's response was pure gold. She gave her daughter, my wife a look while saying a word, or two, that was so condescending with just a touch of dismissiveness, implying that my wife was an idiot. My wife became greatly offended. I witnessed this interaction while sitting at the kitchen table and I almost fell out of my chair laughing internally. I was delighted when I watched this because I immediately recognized what was being reflected was exactly the way my wife offended me and how I offended her.

Later that evening when in the privacy of our bedroom I carefully brought it up to my wife and she'd already got it! Each one of us was doing the same thing to each other, including two generations of women. It was great to witness my wife and her mother because I wasn't involved emotionally with that particular conversation, so I could be objective for the first time and see how she was doing it and how I must be doing it too.

Once I saw it happen between my wife and her mother, I could see it in myself. I then could move forward to deleting it from my programming using The Mirror. Sometimes old habits don't end all that cleanly. Every once in a while, it will come up again and we catch it immediately, both laughing about it. Laughing about it is a completely different energy than being repulsed by it. Here is how I answered the questions for myself to be able to see it clearly.

Projection

Question: What was this person saying or doing that disturbs me?

Answer: My wife gives me a look,and says a couple of words being rude and dismissive, implying that I am an idiot.

Reflection

Question: Where do I say or do the same thing, or think about saying or doing this same thing?

Answer: I had a particular response that my wife found disturbing. I wasn't even aware of it until I saw it through her mother. Once I saw it being done by her mother, I was able to recognize it in myself and stop it. The truth is that sometimes I forget or my wife forgets and we do it to each other again. The difference now is that we can laugh about it instead of being so offended.

So what do we do with this information? Once we recognize that we are disturbed, then we can move on to the third and final step of The Mirror which is the next chapter. Sometimes just seeing how we affect others and are affected is enough for us to choose to stop the behavior. In the example I just gave, I chose to not continue the behavior. I didn't like it when it came toward me and I did not want to make anyone else feel that way. I don't want to be that kind of person. Ultimately I was thankful for this being shown to me, because I want to be my better self.

This story is a great example of how an attitude or

behavior can be generational. We may pick up a behavior from a parent or guardian while growing up that's not who we desire to be, but we're unconscious of that trait until we look in The Mirror. Now it's time to proceed to the third and critical step of The Mirror.

FORGIVENESS: STEP THREE

> The way we experience the world around us
> is a direct reflection of the world
> within us.
> —Ritu Ghatourey

This is the most important step to understand because forgiveness through The Mirror is so different from what you may have done before. Let's begin with the definition of forgiveness. The commonly held definition involves letting someone off the hook, releasing all the resentment, anger, frustration, or harm done to oneself by another. I don't want to spend another second on that traditional definition of forgiveness because that won't get us anywhere in this work. What will help is understanding that in The Mirror, forgiveness is the opposite of what we've all been taught it is.

The person you will be forgiving is yourself. Since everyone in our life is reflecting to us what our consciousness is projecting—reflecting what we are thinking both consciously and subconsciously—then it stands to reason that the only person to forgive is the one who is projecting:

yourself. Forgiveness has everything to do with you and nothing to do with the other person. The person in front of you that is causing your disturbance is there to show you what you need to forgive within yourself.

What forgiveness means in this work is to *give forth* from yourself that which you find so disturbing in another person. To let yourself off the hook (for the things done or thought by you) that the person in front of you is reflecting to you. Because everyone you see is a reflection of you. I'll repeat this a few times because it is absolutely critical to understand and digest.

It is your spouse, children, friends and coworkers who reflect to you how you are thinking and behaving, and that which is in your consciousness. It is your friends, mates, and the people you spend time with regularly who are reflecting to you what you need to forgive within yourself. You don't need to forgive them for showing/reflecting it to you. Start taking back your power by forgiving yourself. What happens when you forgive yourself is that the other person simply stops the behavior that was so disturbing to you—or you just don't notice it anymore because it is now meaningless to you. Hang in there because I will give you some very specific ways of "giving forth" or forgiving that my wife and I have used very successfully throughout the years.

There is no reason to tell the other person that you were offended, disturbed, or mad at them. They've done you a favor because they reflected that information/disturbance to you for you to use to clean up your own consciousness. You have the power to change, grow, and forgive yourself. You are strong enough to evolve your consciousness by watching what disturbs you and then using that information to forgive it within yourself. You will get the benefits. You will gain the energy. You will free your life to be the best you possible.

To be honest, I still get upset when my wife or daughter or someone close to me reflects something very disturbing to me. My emotions jump way ahead of my reason. Even though I'm upset and maybe even yelling, protesting, or demanding some change in the other person, I know in the back of my mind that it's my own self that needs to change. I will jump emotionally and then rant and rave. And when I've calmed down I'll apologize to that person. Next, I will do my own forgiveness work on myself for whatever issue was disturbing me so much.

I have found forgiveness to be a very personal journey. What works as forgiveness for one person may not be right for another. Forgiveness is an inside job, a tailor-made job, there is no single process for everyone. There are so many times when I see something that is disturbing me being reflected by a friend, and I recognize the flaw is within me and I can forgive it immediately because I know that flaw is not who I want to be—that's not my best self. I see the lesser act and I know I've been doing or thinking that same lesser act. It's ugly and I get it. I don't want to be like that and I vow to never again do it. Case closed.

A good example of this happened when my family traveled to Mexico and Belize and then Guatemala. One morning my wife was making a movie of me on her phone as I hailed a taxi to take us to the Guatemalan border. I was being my usual self: thinking that I had to get the best price from a taxi driver. I would pass one driver after another, taking only enough time to discover what they would charge us for the ride.

Later, when I took the time to look at my wife's video, I saw a man, myself, being rude and dismissive, treating people like they were machines. I was shocked watching myself. I felt ugly. I instantly realized this is not the man I intend to be and the pain from the ugliness was motivating enough for me to forgive myself instantly. I recognized that those taxi drivers are just worthy human beings making a living as best they can. From that day on, I began to appreciate each taxi driver; I thanked them and I still negotiated what I thought was an equitable fare. In short, I projected onto my wife's video a very disturbing picture of how I was treating other human beings. Using The Mirror I saw that my reflection was disturbing enough to motivate me to change my ways and forgive myself immediately.

Not all my forgiveness work for myself has been that quick! So I want to share with you a forgiveness process that my wife and I have used which has worked very well for us for years. The process is called Ho'oponopono and it's made popular by Dr. Hew Len. It includes a circle of four simple statements with reflection after each statement. It may be useful for you, so I have included links at the back of the book to Dr. Hew Len's forgiveness process and I recommend it to give you a specific method for self-forgiveness. Remember that forgiveness is like a tailor-made suit and what works for one person may not work for another; Dr. Hew Len's process is just one option.

Ho'oponopono originally was a Hawaiian practice of reconciliation and forgiveness. Dr. Hew Len, a therapist in Hawaii, was called in to help at the Hawaii State hospital where the mentally ill patients were totally out of control. The ward where they kept the criminally insane patients was a dangerous place. Psychologists quit on a monthly basis and the staff would call in sick a lot or simply leave. People would walk through the ward with their backs against the wall because they were afraid of being attacked by the patients. It was, clearly, not a safe place to work.

Dr. Hew Len, an expert in the spiritual practice of Ho'oponopono, was asked if he would work there and see what he could do. So he worked there for three years, and by the end of that time the ward was closed because all the patients had healed. He never saw any of the patients professionally or counseled them; all he agreed to do was review their files. While he studied their files, he would work on himself—he would repeat a mantra over and over—and miraculously, gradually all the patients began to heal. After a few months of Dr. Hew Len being there, patients who had been shackled started earning the right to walk freely. Others who'd been heavily medicated started getting their medications reduced. And those who had been diagnosed as having no chance of ever being released were being freed.

Not only that, but the staff began to enjoy coming to work. Absenteeism and turnover disappeared. They ended up having more staff than they needed, since patients were being released and all the staff were showing up to work every day. What happened to change things so dramatically?

Dr. Hew Len said he was simply cleaning the part of me that I shared with them." The only way I can explain it is this: Ho'oponopono recognizes we are all part of one consciousness, and as such, everything that is in our experience is affected by our actions/reactions. We are responsible for everything we experience! Dr. Hew Len explains, "Total responsibility for your life means that everything in your life, simply because it is in your life, is your responsibility. In a literal sense, the entire world is your creation."

The mantra he used to change the lives of all these criminally insane people was very simple:

Please forgive me...I'm sorry...I love you...Thank you

He was addressing the aspect of his consciousness he shared with that person. The fact that this person was in his experience meant that they shared a part of the same consciousness. So if this other person was suffering, that meant a part of him was also suffering and needed healing. By addressing that aspect of himself, and giving love to it and accepting the Infinite's unlimited unconditional love, the aspect would be healed. He would then just thank the Infinite for healing that problem. With each repeat of the mantra, he would address a new layer, going deeper and deeper until the healing manifested and he felt a deep change and sense of peace within. Let me give you an example of how my wife uses this process and how I used this process differently. Once she recognizes that she's disturbed, she will begin repeating the Ho'oponopono four phrases: I'm sorry; Please forgive me; I love you; I thank you. She trusts that whatever needs to be revealed to her will be, so she continues on with the four phrases, feeling and sensing internally, going deeper until she feels a sense of peace. I, on the other hand, will take a moment after recognizing that I am disturbed and identify the issue that needs forgiving and *then* begin the four phrases of Ho'o-ponopono, again listening and feeling deeply until I feel a sense of peace internally. Let's say that a mutual friend of ours is with my wife and I and that friend lies. We both know that he's lying. My wife will begin the four phrases at her earliest opportunity and trust that what needs to be revealed for her will be revealed as she continues the four phrases. I, on the other hand, at my earliest convenience will say to myself, "Where am I lying or deceiving others or myself?" I believe the answers are always close and the answer does always come. I then begin the four phrases and repeat them slowly, sensing myself internally until peace is felt. Both my wife and I have used this technique frequently with The Mirror with great success. So, how do you know when you are disturbed besides the obvious internal agitation? If, when you are talking with a friend or acquaintance and you want to get away from that person, that's a great big red flag. An example of this comes from my wife. She would chat with one of the other mothers while my daughter was participating in an activity. She told me this other mom complained a lot and my wife said she wanted to get away from her frequently but had to see the other mom because of the activity. My wife decided to do her own forgiveness work about complaining, without even identifying where she was complaining internally. The very next time she saw this woman she noticed the woman was no longer complaining while in her presence. That's a great example of how to use The Mirror. Another red flag for being disturbed is to notice when you are gossiping about one person to another person. The point is to catch yourself when you are disturbed and forgive yourself for what's being reflected to you. Whichever way you decide to forgive yourself will be your personal choice. You'll know that you have truly forgiven yourself when the disturbing information disappears. The person that was disturbing will no longer say or do that thing. Or you simply will not notice it any longer. Be honest with yourself and don't disassociate from your emotions by telling yourself this doesn't bother you. The best and the toughest news is that the universe has no problem showing you the same issue again and again and again from one person to another to another until you get it and forgive it. You will have multiple chances to truly forgive an issue because you will continually attract it to yourself. But you do get to choose when you decide to handle it within yourself and for yourself.

Let's say, for example, that you have a good friend whom you love and who has lots of great qualities. The one thing you find disturbing about your friend is that he gossips. You've said to yourself time and time again that you never gossip like your friend. But The Mirror is reflecting to you that you *do* gossip, if not out loud then within your mind. If not, how could that person be gossiping in front of you? Your mind may deny it, but your reflection is telling you the truth. A friend who gossips in front of you repeatedly means you are a gossiper. The fix is not to distance yourself from your friend but to lean into your own mind and dig deeper. You don't have to be gossiping out loud: you could be gossiping in your mind.

You can begin repeating the Ho'oponopono four phrases immediately or wait until you are by yourself. Listen into yourself and notice how you're feeling. The freedom comes in seeing where you think or behave like the person that's disturbing you and then forgiving yourself for that. This information is often deep in your subconscious but it will come up for you to forgive. You'll know you are on it when you feel a change in yourself, in your heart. Once an issue is truly forgiven it will disappear, freeing up tremendous energy and increasing your chances to live life largely.

Don't get discouraged if the same issue comes up later. Old mental habits may linger or you may fall back into that old habit of thinking. You've recognized it in yourself before and so it will be easier to see it this time. Buck up and do your work. Go deeper, because your best self is worth it!

"Fourteen Years Later"

It was about seven in the morning on a cool Florida day when my wife and I woke up knowing that today was our family trip to Busch Gardens. My wife was very excited because The 5th Dimension, a band with a lot of soul, was performing that afternoon. My thirteen-year-old daughter was always excited about the roller coasters at Busch Gardens. But I wasn't feeling excited at all because I'd had a very rough, sleepless night and was already worn out at seven in the morning.

I rolled over and said to my wife in a cranky and demanding tone that we couldn't go that day because I had not slept at all. I told her we'd go tomorrow. I was not considering that she had planned this trip for over a month and she might not be available the next day. She hesitated to agree with me. I then followed up with, "If I can't go and have fun, you can't go and have fun. I wouldn't leave you behind if you hadn't slept." Now, what I thought I had nicely said was, "Gee, honey, I haven't slept at all. Can't we wait and go on another day?" Oh, by the way, "You can't go and have fun if I can't go and have fun!" and that I would never leave her behind.

That set my wife off because fourteen years earlier I had indeed left her to fend for herself during her high-risk pregnancy so I could travel to Egypt and Kenya for my spiritual studies multiple times.

In that moment she flipped out, lost it, and started yelling at me about things I had done fourteen years ago when she had been pregnant with our daughter. I mean, she was really gone and I recognized that. I moved from the bed to the bathroom to catch my breath, but within seconds she was in my face in the bathroom. All I could do at that moment was to leave the house as quickly as possible. My head was spinning as I exited my house heading for a coffee shop.

Somewhere in that heated vortex, she told me she had

been deeply hurt fourteen years ago. She felt that I had abandoned her to go have fun in Egypt and Kenya during her pregnancy—she was forty-two years old at the time and was having a risky time pregnancy due to fibroids. She had not forgiven me for that trip, even though she thought she had, because it came up again. As I drove to the coffee shop in a sleepless daze I tried to make sense of what happened. Her reaction was so extreme that I knew this information/reflection was very important for me to look at.

I remembered how my wife became pregnant early in our relationship and how we both struggled through very tough times with a lot of fear. The warnings from doctors had only compounded our fears. But today my wife was showing me, reflecting to me, that I had not forgiven myself for how I had left fourteen years earlier. I could have gotten mad at her and told her to just let it go—that she was bringing up a really old issue—but that would only be me avoiding my own work, my forgiveness work. Now that the tables were turned, I could finally feel and see a touch of what she must have experienced being left behind when feeling vulnerable.

Until this point, I had always told myself that I'd been terrified because I was in a serious relationship for the first time in my life, and on top of that she was pregnant. I knew that despite my fear I was 100% committed as a father and spouse. I saw those spiritual trips as information and work I needed as a man to be able to stay in a relationship and be a partner and father. I thought I had done my forgiveness work, but now something was different. For the first time, I heard my wife say that she felt I had left her behind when she felt vulnerable.

That was the information I had not heard before, even though she probably had said it numerous times. I owned it and that day they went to Busch Gardens without me. For a brief moment I felt just a bit of that fear about being left behind. Now, one day in Busch Gardens is very little fraction compared to the fear my wife must have felt when I had left the country for two weeks at a time, but I did feel a touch of that fear. I then proceeded to do my forgiveness work: on the fear of being left behind while feeling vulnerable and also on the guilt of leaving one behind while she felt vulnerable.

My revelation was that I had left her to travel to Egypt and Kenya but didn't want to be left behind from Busch Gardens because being left behind didn't feel good. Then I'd tried to control the situation by demanding that they not go, even though I had done the same thing—when it worked to my benefit—fourteen years earlier. This issue had come up a few times in the preceding years and I realized that day I had never gone deep enough to really deal with it.

If the same issue is reflected to you repeatedly, it means there is more in it for you to forgive yourself for. Or you haven't done real forgiveness work to begin with. Don't make yourself wrong, just get back in the saddle and do your work.

I spent the day using the Ho'oponopono technique described above, taking time to feel deeply each statement and what it brought up in me. I went slowly and repeated it several times because it was clear to me that the work I had done previously on this issue hadn't gotten the job done. With Ho'oponopono, I let each statement settle in and feel it deeply, and then I would do it again and again. These were very deep hurts and just recognizing them wasn't going to do the job.

When my ladies returned that night, I didn't say a word about what happened. There was no point in saying anything because my wife was showing me my own unforgiven guilt. Over the next couple of days, I could see my forgiveness work had done the job as her attitude improved and we returned to loving each other.

Projection

Question: What was this person saying or doing that disturbs me?

Answer: She's attacking me for things I thought I had to do fourteen years ago, saying that I had left her behind multiple times when she was feeling vulnerable.

Reflection

Question: Where do I say or do the same thing, or think about saying or doing it?

Answer: I had been attacking myself, feeling guilty for things I had done fourteen years ago while my wife was pregnant, even though I thought I had forgiven those things. She was showing me the guilt in my mind and it wasn't until I went deeper that I could see the issue in a new light.

Forgiveness

Question: What was my forgiveness work?

Answer: I took plenty of time and dug deep in my mind, heart, and soul. I used the Ho'oponopono technique repeatedly throughout the day. I focused on what it felt like to be left behind while feeling vulnerable.

Now it is your turn by simply following the steps of The Mirror.

Projection

Question: What was this person saying or doing that disturbs me?

Answer:_____

_____

Reflection

Question: Where do I say or do the same thing, or think about saying or doing the same thing?

Answer:_____

_____

Forgiveness

Question: What was my forgiveness work?

Answer:_____

_____

So that is the essence of The Mirror. I want to take a moment to reiterate that forgiveness is an internal process unique to each individual, not a one-process-fits-all. I've shared with you what has worked well for my wife and myself, but you must do you own work and discover what works for you. Forgiveness happens inside of you regardless of the way you get there. It's your willingness to go deep inside, be sincere, be willing to change, and be willing to discover yourself on a deeper level.

GETTING THE MOST FROM
YOUR MIRROR

> The world is a great mirror. It reflects back to
>   you what you are.
> —Thomas Dreier

In this chapter, I will break down four key points that will help you achieve the results you want from The Mirror.

1. Start small
2. Speak from the "I"
3. Detachment vs. Dissociation
4. Don't make yourself or anyone wrong

1. Start small (and close to home)

Choose someone you're with daily or weekly. This should be someone that you like, yet who disturbs you every once in a while, but not your spouse or your children. Family relationships typically have too many emotions attached; the emotions can make it very difficult to see yourself being reflected, and that's essential! Try to choose someone like a friend, or a friend of your spouse, or a neighbor. I'm going to call this Person X. After you rack up some wins using The Mirror, you can move on to your spouse or the people closest to you, but starting small will make it easier to see how effective The Mirror is. As you become more confident, and once you see yourself in a spouse or a parent, the rewards will be most valuable for you. Be brave. Laugh at yourself.

It is so important to choose a Person X who comes into your life up-close and personal. The people that are around us are there for many reasons and one of the most important reason is to assist us in our growth, pleasantly or unpleasantly. Each one of them is a gift, particularly the ones we find most disturbing because they will produce the greatest growth in us.

Don't compare your reflections about Person X to anybody else's because everyone you're close to will reflect back only the observer, like a mirror does. Another person may and often will have a completely different experience of Person X. If you are disturbed by Person X, that means the reflection causing the disturbance is specifically for you to use The Mirror on. Let me give you a real-life example.

"Our Night at the Meditation"

My wife and I mediate with a group once a week at a local coffee shop after hours. This is in a relatively small town where there are almost no homeless people to be seen. In the beginning of one of our weekly meditations a homeless man walked into our group mumbling about how he must find his way to a specific homeless shelter so he could get to work the next day. He repeated the statement over and over mumbling that he must go to work and that he always goes to work. He was completely locked down on the idea blocking out any other opportunities that might have presented themselves.

Now my wife, who grew up in Los Angeles and is therefore quite familiar with homeless people, became very disturbed by this man's incessant mumbling and considered him disruptive and wished he would leave. She found him quite irritating as he repeated his mantra of "I must get to work tomorrow." I, on the other hand, wasn't disturbed by him at all and thought to myself: How the heck did a homeless man show up here tonight? To be honest I was quite interested, thinking that his showing up was such a remote chance that the universe must have put him in this place for a very special reason. I was a bit delighted to see what would ensue.

When we went home that night, my wife told me how disturbed she was by his mumbling repeatedly that he had to go to work to this very specific kind of work. She said that he was so locked down in his position that he completely missed the opportunities around him, specifically that this group of meditators may very well have taken up an offering to give him money to help him. I told my wife I wasn't disturbed by him, but there might be something valuable for her to use The Mirror on.

She did use The Mirror and discovered that she had locked down her own attention into believing that one particular thing had to happen in her business and she'd gotten single minded in envisioning how she could manifest that thing. When she released that tunnel vision thinking, and did her forgiveness work, her business exploded with growth from a direction she had not expected. You see, like the homeless man she also had her attention locked down on one thing. It was work she had done before but very little had manifested from it until using The Mirror on the homeless-man experience. Once she did that, her life changed very quickly. New clients starting calling her requesting her services for a channel of work she had begun a few years earlier but hadn't taken off, until now. The moral of the story is that your experience of a person, particularly your disturbance because of a person, will be for you and you alone. Don't compare, because that won't get you anywhere.

Going back to the coffee shop, the homeless man did finally leave and after meditation the group was talking. A woman spoke up, saying that she had been asked to lead a workshop a couple of times but had said no because she didn't feel worthy. She had some physical ailments and she thought she wouldn't be a living example of what she would be teaching. My wife listened compassionately and peacefully while I, on the other hand, became quite disturbed by what the woman said. I thought to myself: How can you possibly say no when someone is asking for your help specifically? I felt the woman wasn't valuing herself unless she appeared a particular way. I told my wife at home how disturbed I was by this woman. My wife said that the woman hadn't bothered her at all and it might benefit me to use The Mirror on this reflection I was disturbed about. So I did. And I quickly realized that I had been limiting my own opportunities by putting up restrictions, conditions, and expectations in my mind instead of simply being willing to say yes to my opportunities. I hadn't been trusting that the universe knew what it was doing. My metaphor now is "Erect no walls to limit myself."

Projection

Question: What was this person saying or doing that disturbs me?

Answer: She was refusing opportunities because she didn't appear a very particular way. A way that she had made up.

Reflection

Question: Where do I say or do the same thing, or think about saying or doing it?

Answer: I had erected mental walls or conditions that I felt I had to meet before I could be worthy to say yes to opportunities presented to me.

Forgiveness

Question: What was my forgiveness work?

Answer: Using The Mirror I quickly realized what I had been doing against myself and immediately opened myself up to saying yes to every opportunity the Universe presented to me. No restrictions, no conditions, no expectations = FREEDOM

On a practical level, this realization opened me up to writing this book more freely and from a more inspired position. I write when I'm inspired, not when I force myself to write, and I've included many sections that were not in my small plan for this book.

2. Speak from the "I" position

Have you ever heard someone say, "The reality is…" or "Everybody is…" or "The fact of the matter is…" or "People are…" or "Life is…"? They are speaking in general terms and that is a very weak position to speak from. This language is based on general assumptions and/or judgments. Each person's consciousness creates their own reality and as you use The Mirror your own reality transforms. What was your reality yesterday will change immediately as you successfully use The Mirror. Also, speaking about people in general terms dilutes your ability to see yourself being reflected to you clearly.

Speaking from the "I" position is where all your power is. If you use phrases such as, "My reality is…" or "I do this when…" or "My truth is…" or "I am…" or "My life is…", you will be speaking powerfully. I'm not talking about being self-absorbed, I'm talking about being self-aware. Remember the Sherlock Holmes analogy in Chapter 3 and the power of being self-observant and scientific? When you speak from the "I" position, you begin to focus your attention into a laser beam, enabling you to see yourself and what's being reflected to you clearly. You will recognize your judgments and beliefs quicker than ever before. "I did this." "I thought that." "I saw myself being this way or that way." "I said that." "I observed this about myself that I'd never noticed before." You can recognize and own what needs to be forgiven while using The Mirror and you can't change what you cannot see in yourself.

Here are some power-speak examples for you to consider: I am lazy today vs. people are lazy. Those people are takers vs. I'm a taker. The reality is...vs. My reality is... Women are just like that, or men are just that way, vs I am that way. The reality is... vs. My reality right now is...

If my spouse acts a particular way that drives me crazy, I can say to myself, "I drive myself crazy when I think or do..." I can ask "Where is my own thinking driving me crazy?" This way you start to own it and can therefore transform it. When your parents or children do or say something that consistently disturbs you, you can say, "I now see that I do this or think this way." You must speak from the "I" position because your ego will not let you see the flaws in yourself otherwise. The ego will have you believe the issue is in other people. But your reflection is showing that this issue is in you, unequivocally. If you will practice speaking from the "I" position, you will immediately feel the difference. Often just recognizing limited, judgmental thinking is enough to trans-form it. But you must make it specific to yourself.

3. Detachment vs. Dissociation

It is so very important to be engaged in life and relation-

ships of all kinds. Dissociation is a mental process of discon-
necting from one's own thoughts, feelings, memories, or
sense of identity. It is critical to notice when you are
disturbed by another person. Often when someone disturbs
me, I will tell myself I'm not disturbed. But I am disturbed.
My denial is a defense mechanism of my ego. My ego would
have me just project everything out of me and blame, judge,
and ridicule other people. There is nothing helpful or
powerful about that position. For example, my wife may say
something that disturbs me, but I'll deny to myself that I'm
disturbed by it.

Other than the obvious internal agitation you may feel
while you are talking to someone, how do you know when
you are truly disturbed by them? Two ways: When you want
to get away from them during a conversation, and when you
are complaining or gossiping about them to another person.

Now, the beauty of how this universe works is that my
wife will continue the disturbing behavior, or more people
will show up in my life reflecting that same behavior or
language, until I admit to myself that I am disturbed and use
The Mirror to transform it. Dissociation is a common way to
avoid actually recognizing that you are disturbed. It lets you
ignore the freedom and power that you would gain by doing
the forgiveness work. You may say to yourself "That doesn't
bother me anymore." But if you search inside yourself
honestly and go a little deeper, you may feel a disturbance.

The good news is that the universe provides you with a
multitude of opportunities to forgive the same thing until
you really get it. That same thing will show up in another
person and another and another until you have done the
forgiveness work of The Mirror. So don't waste your time
avoiding it.

Detachment, on the other hand is a spiritual principle

and quite different. It's a release from desire and—since desires often don't come true, and unfulfilled desires cause suffering—it's a release from suffering. Detachment is a moment-by-moment, day-by-day process of accepting reality as it presents itself, doing your best to align your actions with what you think is right, and then surrendering to the outcome.

Here's an example of detachment: I had a remodeling business and I made a commitment to myself to do a great job every time, and I followed through with that commitment. I wasn't concerned with where my next job would come from, or how big or small I grew. I would often complete one job without another being scheduled only for a new one to appear quickly. I was detached and therefore my business was free to do what it needed to do without me struggling, or trying to make something happen.

Detachment is not about disengaging ourselves from family, possessions, political activism, friendships, and career pursuits—that would actually impoverish our lives. Engagement with people and places, skills and ideas, money and possessions is our walk of mastery in this world. Without these relationships and the pressure they create, it's hard to learn compassion or to deal with anger, pride, and a closed heart. We can't use detachment as a way to not deal with fundamental issues such as livelihood, power, self-esteem, and relationships with other people. Nor is detachment a synonym for indifference, or carelessness, or passivity.

For instance, how could we fall in love and remain detached? Where do we find the motivation to start a business, write a novel, get ourselves through law school, unless we care deeply about the outcome of what we're doing? I believe the mastery of detachment comes from engaging full-on in the world, giving 100% effort of ourselves, and yet still knowing that the end result will be what it is supposed to be, even when it doesn't look the way I think it should.

Make sure to give yourself lots of credit and praise when you use The Mirror successfully. Sometimes this can be very hard work, so do be proud of your successes. All work and no praise isn't going to keep you moving forward. Laugh, love, and then laugh at yourself some more. Do try to balance the joy with the workload. Being happy with your path is also motivating for the next time The Mirror shows up.

The following story from Daniel is a great example of staying engaged and not dissociating in a conversation, even when he didn't like the direction it went. Daniel stayed present, engaged, and detached from any particular outcome.

"Parents/Son Triad and The Mirror"

By Daniel Chriptopher

We three were standing in the red front doorway with the piano to our right. As Mom, Dad and I were having a discussion, I was expressing my appreciation and goals to grow, learn, and achieve a new path in multiple levels of my life by becoming a certified consultant. This new path would open many doors and potentials in my perception and understanding of my path. While sharing these ideas and goals with my parents, they reflected back to me their doubts and that I wasn't enough or did not have the ability/knowledge to be successful in what I envisioned.

While I was observing my parents' reactions and the negative comments they were making about my idea, I clearly heard an aspect of myself squirming and saying, "Your parent's statements are not true."

In this experience of The Mirror, I was able to see my

subconscious beliefs, doubts, and the questioning of my own abilities.

Projection

Question: What was this person saying or doing that disturbs me?

Answer: When I told them my dreams, my aspirations, they responded with negative statements about my abilities. They criticized me and doubted my talents and strengths.

Reflection

Question: Where do I say or do the same thing, or think about saying or doing it?

Answer: They were reflecting my subconscious beliefs doubting my own abilities, talents and character.

Forgiveness

Question: What was my forgiveness work?

Answer: I stayed detached and therefore didn't erupt into an argument with my parents. I clearly heard my internal voice saying these doubts were not true and I chose to stand with this voice instead of my doubts being voiced by my parents.

How many of us have experienced a similar situation growing up and as adults! We have ideas or dreams that we're so excited about and we tell our parents or peers only to have those dreams dashed because of doubts, fears, or questioning of our abilities. Now we know that our parents or peers were reflecting our own doubts, often subconscious, so we don't have to get mad at them. We can begin to let go of that mentality because they are clearly showing us our own beliefs. Also, this story will help you to understand that there's no reason to make anyone wrong, including ourselves.

4. Don't make yourself or anyone else wrong

It can be easy to make yourself wrong and judge yourself

harshly. It's critical to not do this, though, because the judging is just another way for your ego to slow your growth. Growth is all about learning, practicing, and then learning again. For 99.9% of the population, this is completely new information and a new way of seeing yourself, your world, and the people in your world. There's no reason to say anything about what is being reflected for you to another person. All the work and all the growth and freedom comes from you, for you, and to you. Each person that is being a reflection of you is there for you. How they see the situation is usually very different and expressed in their own language, and discussing it with them is pointless because this is not a debate. If you are disturbed by another person, that disturbance is for you and you alone.

All that being said, after using The Mirror for ten-plus years there are still times when I blame another person, usually my wife, and tell her about it. My emotional body will throw a temper tantrum every once in a while. When this happens I don't make myself wrong by saying to myself, "I'm so stupid" or "I should know better." I simply recognize what has happened and if I feel it's warranted, I will apologize to her. I give myself a few minutes to get into my right mind and proceed using The Mirror.

Your ego can and will distract you every time if you let it. It will have you blaming others for your situation and your disturbances. It will try to keep you from seeing and understanding your reflections. It will swear that the problem is the other person, not you, and then launch into a myriad of reasons to criticize the other person. Accepting responsibility for your reflections will tame your ego and that's a very good thing. Every person in your presence is going to show you something you're still holding in your consciousness.

Do your best to keep your mouth shut and do your own work with The Mirror. If you do, you will see that person change in front of your eyes and they'll never know anything happened. As they are your reflection you become a reflection for them as well. And if they are interested, great. And if they aren't interested, leave it alone so they can be a clear and clean mirror for you.

A great example of "keeping my mouth shut" is in the story about my wife, her mother, and myself in Chapter 5. I saw my wife's mother give my wife "the look," and recognized what was happening. There was no reason to say a thing to her mother. She's not interested in The Mirror and at 80-plus years old she is free to think and do as she likes.

All right, it is your turn to use The Mirror again for the evolution of your consciousness.

Projection
Question: What was this person saying or doing that disturbs me?
Answer:_____

_____

Reflection
Question: Where do I say or do the same thing, or think about saying or doing the same thing?
Answer:_____

_____

Forgiveness
Question: What was my forgiveness work?
Answer:_____

_____

GETTING MORE GAME

> Everyone and everything that shows up in
> our life is a reflection of something that is
> happening inside of us.
> —Alan Cohen

Advanced Mirror Distinctions

As you master the basics of using The Mirror for your freedom and growth, you can move into the advanced stages. The advanced stage of mastery in using The Mirror is to add more distinctions into what you're projecting, reflecting, and forgiving from your consciousness. Remember that everything you see in the physical world is a reflection of your consciousness.

Your Children as Your Mirror

Your children may well be the clearest and most direct reflection of your consciousness. And the younger they are, the clearer they will reflect your consciousness to you. Because we love our children so much, we are highly motivated to do the best for them. Our greatest blind spots will be revealed by our children because our relationship with them is unique: typically they won't censor themselves in our presence. By *censor* I mean they won't avoid criticizing you, pointing out those places you'd like to avoid looking at within yourself. Co-workers and friends may censor themselves due to social pressures to be polite, to be liked, and non-confrontational. Even relatives will often censor themselves, depending on the culture in which they grew up. An example of this is that my parents never brought up anything until it reached a crisis level. They would go on and on silently as trouble was brewing, but never said anything until it exploded.

Even our spouses, knowing our pressure points, may avoid talking about an issue they know we are sensitive about. But our children are uninhibited, uncensored, and therefore a crystal-clear mirror of our own consciousness. They don't care about our feelings in the same way that a spouse, co-worker, or friend will. My daughter will show me things that my wife won't, and my wife will show me things that a friend or a co-worker won't.

Allow me to give you an example. Lately my daughter has taken to picking at me. We have always wrestled each other, so it's not unusual for us to go after one another. But I've found myself disturbed about a particular activity she recently began. I'm an older parent and she pulls at my skin, or makes fun of my skin sagging and even points out the hair growing out of my ears. Now, a comment about this every once in a while from her would not catch my attention, but she has been relentless! She's definitely catching my attention and causing a disturbance within me.

I could get mad at her and scold her, telling her she's being insensitive or I could stop playing with her, but that would be making "her" the problem and with The Mirror we know she's not the problem, she's my reflection. My judgments about getting older are the problem. I must admit that I have noticed I have negative judgments about getting older. I have noticed a critical voice within my head complaining to me about the sagging skin on my neck and the new hairs growing on my ears. I have also witnessed this internal voice in my mind that is criticizing other people who are older than myself. So using my daughter and The Mirror, I've realized I'm not so cool about growing older.

These judgments create disturbance and pain within me. Now I'm using The Mirror anytime this shows itself to me because I want to embrace myself at every age. And now I can say I'm glad my daughter reflected my ageism so I can transform it and be happy and peaceful within myself. And, just as importantly, I want to love my daughter and wrestle with her freely. Remember, the person reflecting to you is never the problem.

The younger the child is, the less likely they are to "behavior-modify" themselves for you. They are just being authentic and they can be extremely honest at times. It's not always what your child is saying, but also how they are being with you. Is your child being stubborn or flexible, happy or angry, truthful or dishonest, sick or well? However you perceive them will be a reflection of your own consciousness.

Parents often complain about their kids doing things they don't like; we try to control the child's behavior by punishing the child. Complaining is a form of disturbance. But each time the parent is annoyed, the parent is doing the same thing the child has done: that's how our consciousness reflects back to us. If the parents would see that annoying trait in themselves and use The Mirror on themselves, they would free themselves from their own bad behaviors. That parent would become a better person, while the kid's behavior would change without any punishment or even a conversation.

Adults often try to set all these rules and controls on kids because it is all they know and have known. Let's say, for example, that you have a parent who's aggressive, a bully of sorts. That parent's child starts to be a bully by being aggressive at school, the child gets into trouble, and a school counselor is called in. The parent and school system try to control the child by punishment, grounding the child or inflicting other sorts of controls. But all along the child has been reflecting something that's going on in the house, specifically in the parent or guardian. The child cannot change, because the cause is the parent who's being a bully. If the parent would use The Mirror their child is showing them, and forgive themselves, the child would be released from this "bullying" energy and change automatically.

I've heard parents complain about their own or other children being too "cliquish:" isolating from others in a small, exclusive group. Yet I know the parents have with-drawn to a small group of friends or family, in essence isolating themselves. The parents will continue to see the child or other children as being "cliquish" or "isolating" until the parents see it within themselves and change. A parent or school administrator can impose "controls" on a child all day long, but it will not solve the problem because it is the parent or guardian who has the issue that needs to be transformed.

So if you have a child begins stealing, you can punish that child and deliver lectures, but if you begin to see where you are "taking," you'll be using a more powerful tool. You can free yourself using The Mirror and the child will change without ever being spoken to, or punished.

I do believe we all do the best we can with the information we have. Parents, teachers, counselors, and guardians just don't know this information, yet, and are therefore doing what they have known in the past. I believe the best we can do is to free our children from dealing with our own stuff by using The Mirror to clean ourselves up. If we can manage that, not only are our kids released to be themselves freely, but our own life energy is released within us so that we can be more healthy, wealthy, and free.

So what is your child reflecting to you currently that you find disturbing? Only you can answer that—your child may disturb you with one thing and then behave differently with another parent. Or you may be disturbed by your child and the other parent is not disturbed at all. This is a completely personal experience and only you can know when you are disturbed internally. It is critical that you look deeply into yourself when disturbances happen.

I've given a great example of one parent being disturbed while the other isn't bothered at all. Do you remember my previous story about my ageism judgments? I was very disturbed when my daughter would pick at me about getting older, pulling on my sagging skin or pointing out the hair growing out of my ears. But my wife wasn't disturbed when she witnessed this and my daughter doesn't pick at my wife about these sorts of things. Clearly I was disturbed about getting older and my wife wasn't because I held the negative judgements about growing older.

Both my wife and I have been disturbed that my daughter talks so little or not at all about her feelings. Yet, as I have earlier stated, I grew up in a family that never talked about such issues until they were at a crisis stage. Hmm?

My wife has told me that her family was the same way: no talk about personal issues, feelings, or the deep stuff. So why am I even the least bit surprised that my daughter isn't talking? It is time for me to stop complaining and start using The Mirror on myself.

Does your child have physical illnesses such as tummy aches? Let my wife tell you a story from her experiences in 2014.

"What Does a Mole on My Husband's Face Have to Do with My Daughter's Stomach Aches?"

by Sandra Jones-Keller

Recently my very healthy and fit daughter has been having a lot of stomach aches. Foods she has eaten for years now suddenly upset her stomach after one small bite. She's a bit sluggish and whiny and has a hard time getting through a meal.

I briefly considered taking her to a doctor, I was getting so concerned. But instead, I turned to spiritual principles to look at what is going on in my household that might be upsetting her. According to Louise Hay (one of my go-to gurus) stomach and intestinal problems have to do with dread, fear of the new, or not feeling nourished. Well, it wasn't too difficult to identify the problem.

Back up to about six months ago. My husband had a small mole on his face that came out of nowhere. He has lots of moles, so at first it was no big deal. We kept watching it for changes and noticed that it was odd-looking, not smooth like his other moles but kind of flakey. Around a month ago, I finally insisted he get it checked out. Two opinions suggested that he have a biopsy done on it. That's about the time my stomach tightened with a sense of dread. Thomas was nervous as well. We told our daughter Mecca the reason for Thomas's sudden and frequent visits to the doctor, while trying to keep it light so she wouldn't worry.

The closer we got to his biopsy date, the more frequent her stomach aches. Even though our words were light, she was picking up on our fear energy, which was outpicturing as her stomach aches. I worked with her on deep breathing and grounding techniques—which helped quite a bit—all the time recognizing that as long as we were afraid she would be also.

The biopsy confirmed our worst fears: melanoma skin cancer, the most serious and aggressive type. It can spread to other parts of the body and get in the lymph nodes. It was difficult for me to stay grounded for a few days because my dad had just passed away from cancer a couple of months ago and my mind kept drifting to my greatest fears. I finally pulled myself together, realizing that my husband is not my ailing father and his diagnosis is very different.

Thomas had his outpatient surgery one week ago and we got the all-clear last Thursday that he is cancer-free! His energy shifted immediately—calmer and more peaceful—as did mine. My insides feel settled for the first time in a month. It's now been four days since the all-clear and Mecca's stomach aches have completely disappeared. She's eating most of the food on her plate again and hasn't once said, "Mommy, my tummy hurts" in that sad voice with sad, almost teary eyes. She's returned to the happy and carefree child that I know her to be! Her stomach aches were simply mirroring back to us our fear about Thomas's mole. Better to have worked this out than make an unnecessary trip to the doctor!

[The following is my wife's voice using The Mirror.]

Projection

Question: What was this person saying or doing that disturbs me?

Answer: My daughter was not feeling well, having frequent stomach aches, which were very unusual for her.

Reflection

Question: Where do I say or do the same thing, or think about saying or doing the same thing?

Answer: Her stomach aches made me realize how terrified I really was about what would happen to Thomas. I thought I was handling things okay until my daughter showed me the truth. And since my dad passed away from cancer a few months before, my fears and sensitivity were heightened.

Forgiveness

Question: What was my forgiveness work?

Answer: I had to use the four phrases of the Ho'oponopono forgiveness process because I wasn't even clear of everything that I was afraid about. By going through the process repeatedly, I was able to digest the information and saw that my daughter's stomach aches disappeared.

My wife's real life story demonstrates how our daughter was reflecting my wife's difficulty digesting the diagnosis of Melanoma that I received from the dermatologist. Next, here's a story from my own life demonstrating how I was able to use The Mirror to immediately transform a cold into vibrant health in my daughter.

"My Baby Daughter as My Mirror"

In 2000 we were living in Atlanta, Ga. My daughter Mecca was a toddler and I took her with me to visit my parents in Kentucky while my wife traveled to California to visit her own parents. Both of my parents loved Mecca, my daughter very much and enjoyed being with her. It was a thrill for us to spend time together and I thought I could use my parents' help since I was parenting a toddler by myself during that trip. On our first day there, I noticed myself slipping into the kind of thinking I did when I was a child: I was taking on a childhood role that I didn't like and had thought I was long done with. I watched myself start to listen to my mother as if she were an authority figure, not an equal, when I myself was the parent at this moment.

On the evening of that first day, I was preparing Mecca for bed and I noticed she was coughing a bit. My mom said, "She must be catching a cold. We'll get some medicine for her tomorrow because there's a lot of that stuff going around now." I said goodnight to my mom and went to the bedroom Mecca and I would sleep in.

As I sat on the edge of the bed looking at Mecca, I thought about what Mom had said. Then, more importantly, I thought about what Mecca was reflecting to me. As I thought deeper, I realized Mecca's coughing (sickness) was reflecting to me my own sick thoughts. Specifically, I had begun to think the way I had when I was a child; I was taking on the childhood role I'd played some 50 years ago. I didn't feel powerful, clear, or fully conscious. I knew my childhood role was not who I currently was and I vowed in that instant that I was strong, clear, powerful, and alive with Spirit. I felt strong and confident as I went to sleep.

When I awoke in the morning I felt great and very clear in my thinking. More importantly, Mecca felt great. There was no cough, no cold, nothing but vibrant health. My mom entered our room ready to administer cough medicine and stopped in her slippers. She simply could not believe my daughter wasn't sick and said so in amazement. I could believe it, and I knew why she had started coughing the night before and why she was vibrantly healthy in the morning. I had straightened out my mind and never said anything else about it to my mother.

Projection

Question: What was this person saying or doing that disturbs me?

Answer: My daughter was coughing like she was catching a cold.

Reflection

Question: Where did I say or do the same thing, or think about saying or doing it?

Answer: Being with my parents, I had regressed into a role I had played as a child myself. I was thinking weak, sickly thoughts.

Forgiveness

Question: What was my forgiveness work?

Answer: I recognized that I had regressed into a childhood role and that I could stop myself. I then said to myself, "That's not who I am now." Next I chose to be the clear-thinking, powerful adult I am now, my true self. That's what it took to express vibrant health again for both my daughter and myself.

Whenever my child is sick I'll look to see what part is sick and what that part symbolizes. The stomach is digesting, the back is support, a cough is wanting to be heard, congestion is confusion, and so on. For details, you may also want to use Louise Hay's book, *Heal Your Body: The Mental Causes for Physical Illness and The Metaphysical Way to Overcome Them.* Her book will give you some insight and direction on where to look, and there's a link to it in the back of this book. There is nothing like my own sick child to motivate me to do my work and clean myself up.

Sick thoughts will produce sickness in the body. If you have read this book this far, I'm sure you're open to this idea. What is a sick thought? Any thought that isn't loving, strong, and clear.

It's your turn to do the process. Let's warm you up by using The Mirror with your child to show you a very positive quality about yourself.

Projection
Question: What is my child saying or doing that inspires me? Answer:_____

_____

Reflection
Question: Where do I say or do the same thing, or think about saying or doing the same thing?
Answer:_____

_____

Forgiveness
Question: How can I appreciate this quality within myself now?
Answer:_____

_____

Now it is time for you to use The Mirror with your child to help you move forward in consciousness and therefore freedom. Write down what's disturbing about your child currently. Maybe your child is giving you one-word responses to all your questions, or you've caught the child taking someone else's money. Possibly the child doesn't listen to anything you say and just wants to do it her/his way. Maybe your child is sick a lot or can't concentrate? Whatever it is that's disturbing you, write it down now.

Projection
Question: What is my child saying or doing that disturbs me? Answer:_____

_____

Reflection

Question: Where do I say or do the same thing, or think about saying or doing the same thing?

Answer:_____

_____

Forgiveness

Question: What was my forgiveness work?

Answer:_____

_____

YOUR OWN BODY AS YOUR MIRROR

> You are a mirror of yourself in others.
>   Whatever you want, give. Be the best
>   reflection of yourself.
> —Karen A. Baqueira

So far we have talked about how your friends, co-workers, boss, spouse, parents, and children are excellent reflections of your consciousness and how you can use that information to transform your own life using The Mirror. Now let's talk about the mirror you are living in, your body. Your body is a reflection of your consciousness being projected into physical form, and you can use that reflection to transform yourself and your body into radiant, vibrant health.

We start with an inventory of what your body is reflecting to you. Are you healthy or sickly? Do you radiate energy or are you tired much of the time? Do you have particular parts of your body that ache, burn, or cause you problems? Do you have a disease or multiple diseases? Are you addicted to smoking, drinking, drugs, sugar, etc.? Is your back a constant source of problems? How do your joints, knees, feet, and hips feel?

An illness or body pain is a symbol for what's really ailing you in your consciousness. A great resource for identifying what the pains and illnesses in different parts of the body are reflecting back to you is the book by Louise Hay entitled *Heal Your Body* and I've put a link in the back of this book to help you find it. It has been in print since 1976 and identifies what a pain or illness can reflect in your thoughts/consciousness. It can and often will point you in a direction that will be beneficial for you to examine.

I believe one must always pay attention to one's own intuition when identifying the thoughts causing illnesses or body pain. Our bodies do out-picture our judgments, beliefs, and thoughts—both conscious and subconscious. Bodily sickness and disease are reflections of sick thoughts. So what are sick thoughts? In my humble opinion, any thoughts or beliefs that aren't loving, generous, kind, powerful, and inclusive are sick thoughts. But that's just my opinion. You have decided for yourself already or you may consider re-evaluating after reading this section.

The location of the pain or illness is a symbol (a metaphor, if you will) that gives you clues into what unloving beliefs and judgments may be in your mind that are hurting you. I am going to give you a few examples from my own life and experiences that I've transformed using The Mirror. My short-lived back problems meant to me that I did not trust my foundation, my core which is my belief in Universe that supports me. The back is a symbol of support on a core level. That meant I'd lost my trust in life, spirituality, and the confidence that I am taken care of by the universe. Using The Mirror, I realized that my foundation, my core strength, was my spiritual support and that I need not do everything myself, that I could trust in something larger than myself. What does you back symbolize for you?

For a while I had skin irritation, dryness, and itchiness which meant to me metaphorically that I didn't feel comfortable in my skin. My skin during this lifetime is Caucasian and in the following story you will understand why I didn't feel comfortable being Caucasian. This is where the Sherlock Holmes analogy in Chapter 3 becomes a very helpful tool for your diagnosis.

I want to share my melanoma story from my viewpoint. My wife's version was shared in Chapter 7, where it is related to our child and using The Mirror. But telling you what that incident meant to me will give you two different perceptions of the same events, and demonstrate how one event can provide multiple opportunities for transformation. This also will give you a powerful example of how I use The Mirror for healing my own body.

"My Body's Melanoma as My Mirror"

My wife began suggesting I go to a dermatologist to have a mole on my face checked out. She repeatedly said she didn't like the look of it. I've had a lot of moles in various places on my body since I was a child, so I didn't think it was a big deal. I've watched moles come out of nowhere and others disappear after years. But she persisted about this point particular mole over a period of one to two years and I finally made an appointment to see a dermatologist for a skin screening.

It was May of 2014, and I was sixty years old. I went to the dermatologist telling myself I was a very physically active, healthy man. I had never had a major disease or a broken bone but I did have the typical ailments as a child including the flu, numerous colds and such, and I'd also had some digestive problems. There was no history of skin cancer in my family except for my sister having a question-able mole removed a few years prior.

The dermatologist checked all my moles from the toes up, but when she got to my face she stopped and said, "We should take a closer look at this tiny mole on your right cheek." This was the same mole that my wife had asked me to take a look at repeatedly over the previous two years. My wife's father had recently died from cancer so my wife was genuinely concerned.

The dermatologist took a biopsy and sent it off to the lab while I went about my day telling myself there was nothing to worry about, and I'm fine and healthy. Early one morning after a week, the phone rang: the dermatologist. She said the results were in and that it was melanoma, the most aggres-sive form of skin cancer, which can spread into your organs. I immediately went numb. She said I should schedule the surgery to have it removed immediately! I was in shock and mumbled questions to her about alternatives but she wasn't having any of it. She said, "This is our protocol." I hung up the phone very much in shock. I was simply trying to accept the information. I called my wife and told her. She sounded as shocked as I was feeling. No surprise, because she was reflecting me. I'd arranged the surgery for a week from then and went about my workday rocked by the news.

I had been using The Mirror for a while with great results. After a bit of time, and I do mean a little bit, I began to look inside myself for what judgments or thoughts I had been holding onto to that would create such a big issue on my face—or should I say, "in my face." The beauty of our bodies is that they will show us where our thoughts and beliefs, both conscious and unconscious, have gone askew. Melanoma is a big deal and extremely dangerous, so I knew I wouldn't have to look far. I just had to be willing to be more honest with myself. And the fact that the mole was on my face meant to me that this issue was in my face metaphorically speaking. Instantly I realized a big judgment that I'd known and ignored for decades. I held terrible judgments against white people, my own race! I believed we were mean, hateful, greedy people more often hiding our hatred underneath a smiling face. I also believed we wanted everybody around us to look the same as we did: white. I secretly hated being white and felt guilty for the privileges I expected from society.

In that instant of being highly motivated, I forgave myself of these judgments and vowed to knock it off completely. I had known of and ignored these judgements for decades. I knew how critical this forgiveness process was because I was facing melanoma. I went ahead with the surgery and it was successful in removing the melanoma, with no spreading detected. The scars on my face were horrific, so I wore a big bandage pad for months. I never thought I would look good again yet I was grateful for the skill and mastery of the doctor and nurses. And just as grateful did I feel inside myself at giving forth these judgments of hate. I had been literally killing myself by holding these judgments.

Well, I healed magnificently! It was gradual, taking months to a year, but my face looks great and I feel great. It's been four and a half years of annual skin screenings with no evidence of any problems. I can honestly say that when something this big happens, to find the problems in my thoughts/consciousness isn't difficult. The urgency of the matter is highly motivating.

Let me pause to say I will utilize every resource such as doctors, chiropractors, acupuncturists, massage therapy, etc. when a problem arises in physical form. I immediately do my forgiveness work and use any and all medical resources to help me straighten myself out. I'll check back in with the medical resource because they will be a source of feedback, a reflection of my consciousness.

Projection

Question: What was my body showing me or doing that disturbs me?

Answer: My body has developed a spot of melanoma and I must have surgery to remove it from my right cheek.

Reflection

Question: What does this symbolize to me? Am I holding judgments or grievances?

Answer: I had been holding very harsh judgments about white people, being one myself. This had gone on for so long that melanoma appeared in my face. I knew I had held these judgments for decades but refused to deal with them until now. The symbolism was that this mole was "in my face," indicating I must look at it immediately.

Forgiveness

Question: What was my forgiveness work?

Answer: I finally admitted that these judgments about myself and other Caucasians were killing me and that I must deal with them now or die. Next, I used Dr. Hew Len's Ho'oponopono forgiveness technique repeatedly until I felt inside myself that I had changed. I swore to myself to never judge another person regardless of race or any other reason. I have noticed, in the years since, that every once in a while I'll catch myself judging another person but will quickly remind myself that love is the only healing element.

In the previous chapter my wife described how during this melanoma scare it was very difficult to digest the information. And in my version of this story I've demonstrated how hateful judgements I had held we're killing me until I changed myself by using The Mirror.

The next story is a demonstration of following my intuition when using The Mirror to transform myself. It is not always so easy to identify my negative judgments that are creating pain. Sometimes I have to completely trust my intuition and follow up doing my own forgiveness work as best I can determine. I will then watch to see if a change occurs and the following story is a perfect example of how this can play out.

"My Wife's Cough and the Money Train"

Starting in January 2012 my wife had a bad cough, sometimes better and sometimes worse. It started shortly after she left her job producing public television fundraising breaks at Georgia Public Television. At times it was so bad it rocked the house and I was very disturbed and concerned about it. I refused to own it for myself as a reflection of my thinking for a long time. But she persisted, on and on and on with the coughing. I finally had to look at it for myself because I knew I was very disturbed by it and she persisted in doing it loudly and with great gusto. I looked at myself and said, "I'm not sick, I don't have a cough or anything physically wrong. I'm healthy. Why does this disturb me so much and why does she keep doing it?"

Well, I needed to dig deeper and was very resistant to doing so until I finally gave in. As I looked at thoughts and beliefs, I realized this "sick" behavior of coughing was a reflection of my "sick" thoughts. So what was the thought I holding that was so sick? I must tell the truth: I was very resistant to being really honest with myself but her coughing was extremely motivating. As I persisted, I had a hit of intuition that my beliefs about money were the problem. Particular my thoughts/beliefs about a lack of money and my sense that there was just enough to get by. Also, I believed that since I made most of our money at that time, I needed to control paying it out. These "sickly" thoughts were being reflected back to me by my wife in the form of coughing. According to Louise Hay, coughing is a crying out or calling for attention.

I followed through using The Mirror and being guided by my intuition. My beliefs about having and using money kept coming up. I had to ask myself if I was ready to let go and trust the Universe would support us? Didn't I have to budget, plan, squeeze every bit out of every dollar? Wasn't it my responsibility to make enough money to keep us comfortable? The answer coming back was "no, it's not your responsibility".

Honestly after years of budgeting, scrabbling and working I was ready to let go of all of my beliefs about money. I did let go! I told myself I would not check the bank balance. I would not budget. I would not use my mine to try to control money another moment! And guess what? It has been the most freeing experience of my life. I had no idea how I had imprisoned my thinking. It's been a few years now and I am so happy about this decision. It has been liberating. And a side effect has been that more money than ever is flowing through our us. Looking back I wonder if all those years I had unconsciously been restricting the flow of money.

Projection

Question: What was disturbing me about my wife's behavior?

Answer: She was having coughing attacks that rocked the walls.

Reflection

Question: Where was I thinking or doing that or what does this symbolize to me?

Answer: I had a hint of intuition that the way I was thinking/controlling/budgeting/ allocating money was my problem and somehow it was associated with her coughing.

Forgiveness

Question: What was my forgiveness work?

Answer: I made a clear decision to release my mental grip on budgeting and controlling our finances down to the last penny. I felt a huge wave of freedom immediately. Shortly thereafter, more money than ever starting flowing into our lives. I'm so happy to be free of my tight, controlling thoughts and behaviors. Most importantly, my wife's coughing attacks ended. I never said a word to her about them or my decision about money until much, much later.

I had to make an intuitive leap and did my forgiveness work on how I was clinching onto money, counting the dollars. I then linked that to my wife's coughing. Based on the forgiveness work I did, I watched my energy change completely about money. I experienced so much freedom internally. It felt wonderful. I also observed that my wife's coughing stopped. And finally, shortly thereafter, I observed that more money was flowing into our family than ever before. Freedom!

Okay, it's your turn to take a look at what your body is reflecting back to you and using The Mirror transform it.

Projection

Question: What is body showing you that is disturbing you?

Answer:_____

_____

Reflection

Question: What does it symbolize or mean to me, or where is my thinking off?

Answer:_____

_____

Forgiveness

Question: What was your forgiveness work?

Answer:_____

_____

Well done. Don't forget to be proud and happy about the improvements you are making in your life!

TRUE TALES FROM LIFE
USING THE MIRROR

> The world is a looking glass and gives back to
> every man the reflection of his own face.
> —William Thackeray

The following is a collection of true-life stories about how
my wife and I have used The Mirror. The first story is about
my wife beginning her "dream job" while being a new
mother and the conflict it created. It is a great example of
how my wife used The Mirror to realize that she felt terribly
conflicted and out of integrity as she began working on a
"dream job" and was a mother to our then very young
daughter. Using The Mirror, she able to resolve her internal
conflict and bring peace, love, and joy to her herself and our
daughter.

"She's Being So Mean to Me"
by Sandra Jones-Keller

As we walked into the deli to grab dinner, my three-year-
old was being mean to me—she wouldn't take my hand, was
totally grouchy, and was just unpleasant to be with. Mecca
and I hadn't spent quality time together in days because of

my busy work schedule, so I was disappointed that our night wasn't going well. I had carved out this evening to catch up and bond with her, and now she wasn't cooperating.

"Mecca, come here!"

"No!" she snapped as she ran ahead of me. I caught her, clutched her hand, which she immediately snatched away from me; it was very unusual for her to run ahead, and more unusual for her to pull away in anger. "Well, if you're going to be mean, we can just go home now!" I was instantly frustrated and exhausted from working too many hours.

Blank stare from her.

"Oh, come on! Really? I just want to have a quick dinner and go home," I thought to myself. I glanced down at my miserable child and realized this was going to get uglier if I didn't change my attitude and demeanor. I took a deep breath, thought for a moment before bending down to look in her eyes.

"Are you mad at Mommy because I've been working so much?"

Mecca burst out crying. I pulled her into my arms, hugged her tightly, and just let her bawl. I finally picked her up, moved out of the entrance to the restaurant, and found a booth for us to sit in.

"I'm sorry I haven't been around lately," I blubbered through my own tears. "I know this is not the agreement we had." She sobbed louder. I wept as I organized my thoughts. People walked by and stared briefly, but left us alone.

"I will take care of this. I have another month left on my contract, so I can't just leave my job, but I will take care of this. I promise I will be around to take care of you again. Is that okay?" She nodded yes and continued to weep. We sat there, holding each other and crying until we were both complete. We finally wiped our tear-strewn faces, blew our snotty noses, ordered dinner, and ate in silence.

When I got home, I told Thomas I would not be renewing my contract—a couple of days later I informed my boss as well. I loved my job! I was the On-Air Fundraising Producer for a public television station. My hours were flexible and Thomas was self-employed, so we co-parented: he worked mornings and I worked afternoons and/or evenings. Mecca spent an abundance of time with each of us.

But this particular pledge drive had been grueling. Management had added several morning shifts, so I was working mornings, afternoons, and evenings. I hadn't seen Mecca in three days at one point because she was asleep when I left in the morning, and was asleep when I returned home late at night. What was supposed to have been a part-time gig had turned into a massive undertaking. During this time, I missed my child and was guilt-ridden for not being around—I went from being a full-time mom to not being home at all. I felt bad because I had deviated from my commitment as a mother, a wife, and a contributing member of my family, but it wasn't until my daughter's emotional breakdown that I saw the damaging impact my job was having on all of us.

It took Mecca a couple of days after this incident to fully warm up to me again, and I was so thankful to have my happy, loving daughter back.

Projection

Question: What is this person saying or doing that disturbs me?

Answer: She was being mean to me, which is out of character for her. She was pulling away, not answering, and didn't want to be with me.

Reflection

Question: Where do I say or do the same thing, or think about saying or doing it?

Answer: I hadn't been around or with her. I completely disappeared because of my work schedule. I was being mean: condemning myself for working too much and being out of integrity with who I said I was. I was feeling guilty about being a bad mom.

Forgiveness

Question: What was you forgiveness work?

Answer: It was multi-layered. First I acknowledged to her that I hadn't been around and apologized to her. Then I made a plan of action to make corrections. Then I practiced Ho'oponopono to let go of guilt for not being around.

Our daughter was reflecting to my wife her own guilt for working so much that she felt she was not being a good mother. Sandra, my wife, got to see through our daughter how mean and critical she was being to herself and to realize that's not the person she wanted to be. My wife made the adjustment that made sense to her at that time. Now, her priorities may change as our daughter grows older. And do note that my wife chose not to renew her contract, which was her decision. Another person may choose other options and be perfectly at peace with their choice. It's a completely individual decision. Remember projection, reflection, and then the final and most important step, which is forgiveness.

The next story is an example of how one can use anything that is disturbing them to bring them more peace and joy. It is a great example of how my daughter's bedroom disturbed me so much that I had to look inside myself.

"My Daughter's Room is Such a Mess!"

When my daughter was very young, my wife and I decided her room would be her room to keep as she liked. It was her space to create the world she wanted and we would stay out of it, as long as she didn't leave food and liquids in there. Well, it must be safe, of course. She's now thirteen years old and throughout her life, she has kept it consistently the same. A MESS!

She has 300 square feet of floor and I can't see one square inch of the carpet because it's completely covered with stuff! Legos, art supplies, art projects, cardboard, clothing, empty glass jars, toys, clothes, ice skates, cloth, fabric, tools, games. What the heck is all of this stuff?

For a long time, I would turn my head away as I walked past her door so I would not see the collage of stuff called my daughter's bedroom. I would deny that it bothered me but I was lying to myself. One time I even took a picture of her sitting in the middle of her room surrounded by a vast array of things obscuring the floor. She was always perfectly at peace with it. She has two large closets and yes, they were filled with stuff as well.

So why did it bother me so much when she was perfectly at peace with it? It wasn't dangerous. It might be dangerous for me to attempt to walk across the floor but she knew where everything was. Again, my wife and I had agreed that her room would be her room to do what she wanted to. What were we thinking? Had we lost our minds when we made that decision? Don't I have to teach her about cleanliness for healthy living? Aren't I supposed to teach her about the benefits of organization? I questioned myself at the same time as I denied that I was disturbed by it.

Clearly, this was my issue and not hers. She loved her room. I judged it harshly. Thank goodness for The Mirror because I recognized it was my problem and did my work. I kept my room fairly neat with beautiful pictures on the walls. I asked myself why I was so disturbed by the way she kept her room and the answer came back loud and clear. Her room appears cluttered because your mind is cluttered. Cluttered with thoughts: hectic, random, uncontrollable egotistical thoughts. Every square inch of my mind was filled with random thoughts.

What did I do upon this realization? I took up meditation again: something I had done for many years but had slacked off on for a while. I remembered clearly the value of slowing down the onslaught of thoughts in my mind. So I picked up my meditations again and peace soon followed.

I am no longer disturbed by the way my daughter keeps her room, for that hasn't changed at all. She loves her room and I love that she loves her room. It's not my style, but so what? Variety is the spice of life, after all.

Projection

Question: What is this person saying or doing that disturbs me?

Answer: She keeps her room filled to the brim with stuff. It feels cluttered, unorganized and out of control.

Reflection

Question: Where do I say or do the same thing, or think about saying or doing it?

Answer: My mind is cluttered with random egotistical thoughts; it's unorganized and out of control.

Forgiveness

Question: What was my forgiveness work?

Answer: It helped just to realize that it was my problem, not hers. Then recognizing the clutter in my mind was motivation enough for me to return to meditating, because it gives me peace of mind, clarity of thinking, and more joy!

Next is my wife's story of how we all can be more powerful and clear in our decision-making by using The Mirror.

"My Daughter is So Busted"

by Sandra Jones-Keller

Last night my daughter was watching Netflix in her room and jumped as I entered. When I looked at the computer screen, it was on the home page. I asked her what she was watching and she said, "My Little Pony." She was acting weird and a little too eager to get rid of me, so I opened Netflix and "The Suite Life of Zack and Cody" came up.

"What's that?" I asked.

"I don't know what that show is. Can you put it back on 'My Little Pony?'" she said, trying to look all innocent.

I knew she was lying, but left her room without making a big deal out of it. I needed to contemplate her lying to watch a children's show. Part of me wanted to lecture her, but a wiser part knew to look at Mirroring first.

Here's how I see Mirroring: If you see it you be it, in a nutshell.

Yuck. Sometimes I really hate The Mirror! I didn't like what I was seeing in Mecca and certainly didn't want to look at that part of me. I like to think of myself as powerful, honest, and certain. Well, Mecca's energy was timid, weird, and secretive.

I set the intention for clarity and guidance before going to bed. That morning during meditation, things became crystal-clear.

A few hours prior to the incident with Mecca, I had offered to give a close friend a promotion code to a website I'm involved in that would give her a free month of membership. As soon as I made the offer, I questioned my integrity. As far as I knew, the promotion code was to be used only during our soft launch, which was a month ago, not a couple of days before our hard launch. To justify my actions,

I'd made excuses in my mind for giving her the code. Bottom line: I felt weird and secretive, the exact same things I was seeing in Mecca.

To remedy the situation, I asked at work if it was okay to give out the code. I received a big yes! Now I didn't have to hide out or make excuses. Time to talk to Mecca.

Our conversation was pretty brief and went something like this:

"Mecca, I want you to be powerful in your life. I feel like you were being really weird and weak when I asked you about 'The Suite Life of Zack and Cody.' Is there any reason why you shouldn't watch that show?"

"I don't know," was her first response. After a little more prodding, she finally admitted she wasn't sure about watching the show because I wasn't familiar with it. We talked about Mirroring and Universal Law and how I had been feeling out of integrity and weird about offering my friend the free promotion code. (Side note. Mecca said, "Yeah, I was wondering about that." She had questioned it as well! Parents: Our children are watching us!)

To conclude, we decided that if we aren't sure about something, we should just ask! It's better to get clarity than hide out feeling we have done something that someone won't like. In my commitment to be clear and powerful in my life, sometimes what shows up are the areas where I'm being the opposite. Thanks to Mecca and using The Mirror, I had an opportunity to be different in this situation.

Parents, what are you seeing in your household that you don't like? The more we can clean up our own stuff, the more peaceful our children will be! How can I rationally lecture Mecca when I'm doing the same thing?

Projection

Question: What was this person saying or doing that disturbs me?

Answer: She was hiding the show she was watching and lied about it. She was acting weird and secretive.

Reflection

Question: Where do I say or do the same thing, or think about saying or doing the same thing?

Answer: Earlier that day I felt weird about giving my friend a promotion code that I wasn't sure was okay to give. It felt weird and secretive. I felt like I could be out of integrity.

Forgiveness

Question: What was my forgiveness work?

Answer: I did the four steps of the Ho'oponopono process until I felt clear and peaceful. After this, I talked to my daughter.

The following story tells how I recognized and transformed my resistance to change and became welcoming of new experiences in my life by using The Mirror.

"Fourteen Years to Realize The Mirror"

When my wife and I had been together for fourteen years, I had a "a-ha" moment. For these fourteen years I have complained to my wife about how stuck she was: how resistant to change she was and how hard I had to work to get her to try new things. Remember, this was my complaint, therefore my projection, and in truth it probably had little or nothing to do with her.

The reflection I was seeing was that it was like pulling teeth to get her to move from Los Angeles to Atlanta, Ga. even though we'd agreed upon that move once our daughter was born. I know that moving is a big deal, but the resistance I saw from her was intense and even though I had been using The Mirror for years I just didn't see where I was resistant to change.

Once, when my wife and I were in Sarasota, Florida at a metaphysical bookstore, I got a reading from a psychic. He told me wonderful things about myself and near the end of the reading he mentioned to me that I didn't like change. I brushed the comment off, but it stuck with me for the next few years. This issue would come up once every few years and went on for years before I finally saw where it was in me.

In my younger years, I'd become a general contractor doing remodeling work, which I loved. But as the years went by I grew tired of the physical part of it and complained to myself and wife, saying I should move into a mental profession before I run out of steam.

Yet I went on remodeling year after year. Finally, an opportunity came along where I could switch over to being a real estate investor. I joined the local investment club, excited about the opportunity, but found myself not attending the meetings regularly. I just didn't have my heart in it and didn't understand why. Then one day I had this Eureka moment. I realized my half-hearted attitude about real estate investing was my own resistance to change, to move forward in my life. The egg had begun to crack.

Then a month or so later, my wife and I were going kayaking and she wanted to go to a new destination. I felt myself tighten up and suggested we go to the same park we always visit. Eureka again! I'd caught myself being resistant to change! I was beginning to see. I stopped myself and changed my mind.

"Let's go to the new location," I said. "I'm seeing my resistance to change and it's ugly," I added. That second event cemented it for me. I could see my resistance clearly and consciously made a decision, using The Mirror to choose differently.

The brevity of this story may not convey the impact of those two moments when I caught myself being resistant. I was the one stuck in the mud. I was the one playing it safe.

Projection

Question: What was this person saying or doing that disturbs me?

Answer: My wife is stuck, so resistant to change.

Reflection

Question: Where do I say or do the same thing, or think about saying or doing it?

Answer: I finally saw within myself how truly stuck I was in my thinking. I was resistant to change and playing it safe, sticking to what I thought I knew and was good at.

Forgiveness

Question: What was my forgiveness work?

Answer: The realization of my resistance to change was powerful enough for me to decide to be different. I've found that often just the realization—the witnessing of myself—is motivation enough to create change. I stand in this new position of flexibility and must stay vigilant in watching my thoughts and old patterns.

Now it is your turn to write yourself a new story for your life.

Pick any person that has created a disturbance in you recently and write it out.

Projection

Question: What was this person saying or doing that disturbs me?

Answer:_____

_____

Reflection

Question: Where do I say or do the same thing, or think about saying or doing the same thing?

Answer:_____

_____

Forgiveness

Question: What was my forgiveness work?

Answer:_____

_____

WHERE DO YOU GO FROM HERE?

> Our environment, the world in which we live
> and work, is a mirror of our attitudes and
> expectations.
> —Earl Nightingale

Congratulations! You have answered the call for a better life. It's your time. So where do you go from here. Remember, practice and grow.

Please do remind yourself often that your own consciousness is being projected outward and reflected back to you moment by moment every day by your family, friends, co-workers and bosses. And most importantly remember that you now know what to do anytime you find your peace is being disturbed. Self-forgiveness is your freedom from the constraints of this world.

Hopefully you have acquired evidence by doing the exercises and if not please go back and follow through with them. I have also left blank pages in the back for you to take notes. Remember to be scientific with you life just like Sherlock Holmes. You will gain evidence that you can use to remind yourself over and over that The Mirror works all the time. Evidence that you can use to motivate yourself during tough times and accelerate your growth during good times.

Love your children and parents and the people closest to you not only because of the love between you but also for what they give to you. They are your greatest gifts because they will show you every last bit of disturbance in your consciousness that you can transform into freedom. Our relationships are the richest, most beautiful gifts we give to each other.

Remember to love your body for it's the only one we have.

I commend and congratulate you for completing this book. This information makes many people fall asleep or become outraged. Either reaction demonstrates that one may not be ready for this and that is perfectly fine. But you are here now. You've made it and hopefully completed the exercises to begin turning the tide in your own life.

Can you imagine a life for yourself of freedom, strength, clarity, calmness, and peace? Can you conceive of a life for yourself living where you want, traveling where you want, enjoying your life freely? Being creative, constructive and courageous. Yes, it is possible and you deserve it as much as anyone, anywhere, at anytime.

Where do you go from here? You may feel that you are alone on an island and most people don't really understand this information if you tell them. But so what? I've found for myself and my wife that it is extremely helpful to have the support of like-minded people to discuss this new way of thinking with. I even have friends that embrace The Mirror and have used it for many years that still feel like they want more like-minded people to talk to. So on the next page, there are links to free support pages such as Facebook and

YouTube. There are also links to workshops I'll be facilitating both online workshops and in person events that I've created to support you on your life adventure.

Your life has taken the fast pass lane into the best life possible lane. Stay on this course and you'll quickly reap the benefits. It doesn't matter where you are in your life. You are never too old or too young to free yourself. You deserve the best possible life just because you are alive!

You can find the current workshop and events schedule at
TheMirrorWorks.com
Email us at TheMirrorWorks@gmail.com
Facebook TheMirrorWorks Facebook Group
YouTube TheMirrorWorks YouTube Channel
Links to;
Sandra Jones-Keller: www.sandrajoneskeller.com
Dr. Carolyne Fuqua: www.circlesoflight.net
Ho'oponopono: Dr. Hew Lin and HoOponopono video
Louise Hay book: Heal Your Body by Louise Hay

Projection > Reflection > Forgiveness Notes

Projection > Reflection > Forgiveness Notes

Projection > Reflection >
Forgiveness Notes

Projection > Reflection >
   Forgiveness Notes

Projection > Reflection >
Forgiveness Notes

71182077R00065

Made in the USA
Columbia, SC
25 August 2019